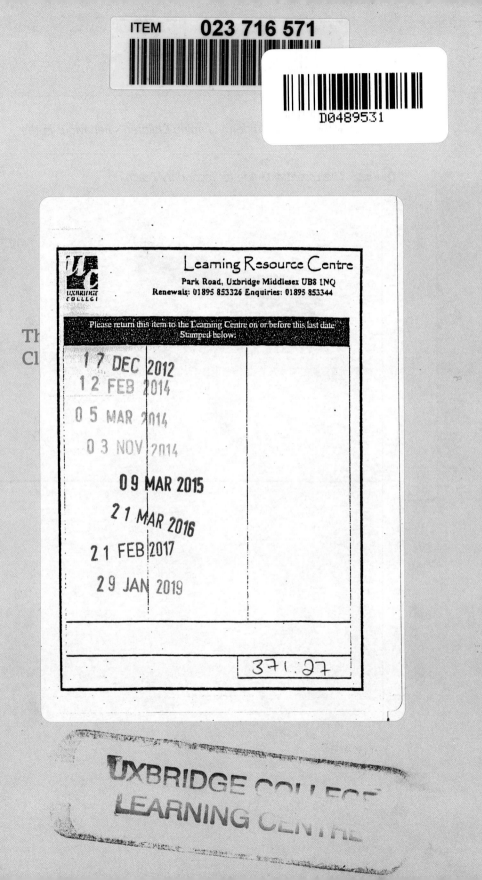

Other titles in the series

Cousins: *The Essential Guide to Shaping Children's Behaviour in the Early Years*

Davies: *The Essential Guide to Secondary Teaching*

Dix: *The Essential Guide to Taking Care of Behaviour*

Dix: *The Essential Guide to Taking Care of Behaviour for Learning Support and Teaching Assistants*

Senior: *The Essential Guide to Teaching 14–19 Diplomas*

Thompson: *The Essential Guide to Understanding Special Educational Needs*

Trant: *The Essential Guide to Successful School Trips*

Walker: *The Essential Guide to Lesson Planning*

Woods: *The Essential Guide to Using ICT Creatively in the Primary Classroom*

The Essential Guide to Classroom Assessment

Paul Dix

**Longman
is an imprint of**

Harlow, England • London • New York • Boston • San Francisco • Toronto • Sydney • Singapore • Hong Kong
Tokyo • Seoul • Taipei • New Delhi • Cape Town • Madrid • Mexico City • Amsterdam • Munich • Paris • Milan

PEARSON EDUCATION LIMITED

Edinburgh Gate
Harlow CM20 2JE
Tel: +44 (0)1279 623623
Fax: +44 (0)1279 431059
Website: www.pearsoned.co.uk

First published in Great Britain in 2010

Pearson Education is not responsible for the content of third party internet sites.

ISBN: 978-1-4082-3025-1

British Library Cataloguing-in-Publication Data
A catalogue record for this book is available from the British Library

Library of Congress Cataloging-in-Publication Data
Dix, Paul.
  The essential guide to classroom assessment / Paul Dix.
     p. cm.
  Includes bibliographical references.
  ISBN 978-1-4082-3025-1 (pbk.)
  1. Educational tests and measurements. 2. Academic achievement--Testing.
  3. Students--Rating of. I. Title.
  LB3051.D575 2010
  371.27--dc22
                          2010005344

10 9 8 7 6 5 4 3 2 1
14 13 12 11 10

Hand-drawn illustrations by Bill Piggins
Typeset in 11/14 pt ITC Stone Sans by 30
Printed and bond in Great Britain by Ashford Colour Press Ltd, Gosport, Hants

For Ellie, Alfie and Bertie

Contents

About the author   viii
Acknowledgements   ix
Publisher's acknowledgements   x
Introduction   xi

Chapter 1 Creating a classroom climate for successful assessment   1

Chapter 2 Autonomous assessment, motivated learners   17

Chapter 3 Teaching metacognition or 'knowing that you know!'   41

Chapter 4 Practical strategies for peer assessment   63

Chapter 5 Negotiated target setting   79

Chapter 6 Pivotal's Negotiated Assessment Grids (NAGs)   95

Chapter 7 Managing active assessment in the classroom   109

Chapter 8 Differentiation and personalisation of assessment   121

           Conclusion   137
           References and additional reading   138
           Index   141

About the author

Paul Dix is a leading voice in behaviour and assessment both in the UK and internationally. As managing director of Pivotal Education he leads a team of ten behaviour, assessment and learning specialists in training and intervention projects. Paul won the UK National Training Award for the South East in October 2009. He is a trainer with an exceptional reputation for designing and delivering training that promotes real change.

Paul trained at Homerton College, Cambridge and has taught in and managed a wide range of schools and colleges. His work was highlighted by HMI and Ofsted as a key component in turning round a school in 'Special Measures'.

Paul co-founded Pivotal Education in 2001. As the lead trainer, Paul has trained teachers, lecturers, youth workers, advisers, students, mentors and classroom assistants in early years to adult education. His work on behaviour and assessment is used successfully in colleges, schools (both mainstream and special), PRUs and initial teacher training programmes.

His Taking Care of Behaviour and Managing Extreme Behaviour courses have both been featured as 'Course of the Week' in the *Times Educational Supplement* magazine.

Paul is author of the Government's New Deal Mentor Training Programme. His work has been featured on ITV, Teachers' TV and in the *Times Educational Supplement*. His first book, the *Pivotal Behaviour Management Handbook*, was reviewed in the *Times Educational Supplement* as 'This is a terrific book'.

Paul is a columnist for *Teach Primary!* magazine, contributes regularly to the *Times Educational Supplement* and has been featured in the *Guardian*.

You can keep up to date with Pivotal's work on the Pivotal Behaviour blog, at www.pivotaleducation.com/behaviour/blog.php. You can book Paul for training and keynote speaking by emailing ellie@pivotaleducation.com.

Acknowledgements

I would like to thank Joe May for his permission to include the Negotiated Assessment Grids. Joe and I have worked together for many years as both teachers and trainers. Much of the practice that has been included in this book is practice that we developed together in some of the most challenging circumstances.

Thanks also to Karen Brown from Bournville School in Birmingham. Karen's materials appear throughout the book and reflect outstanding practice. Karen has helped in the drafting, review and refinement of the practical strategies within this book.

Finally thank you to Ellie for organising the rest of our lives while I spent long hours deep in the writing bunker.

Publisher's acknowledgements

We are grateful to the following for permission to reproduce copyright material:

Figure 2.1 adapted from *The 7 Habits of Highly Effective People* by S.R. Covey, Copyright © 1989, The FranklinCovey Company; Figure 3.4 Copyright © Belle Wallace 2000; Figure 5.3, the Special Mission Card text on pages 88–9 and the Personal Profile exercise on pages 125–6 Copyright © Karen Brown 2009, Expressive Arts Department, Bournville School and Sixth Form Centre, Birmingham; Table on page 101 adapted from 'The 10 Principles: Assessment for Learning',Qualifications and Curriculum Development Agency (QCDA).

In some instances we have been unable to trace the owners of copyright material, and we would appreciate any information that would enable us to do so.

Introduction

As a teacher I want to be able to reflect on not just what I am delivering but how effective my teaching is, what skills my students have learned, how well they comprehend concepts and how much they understand. I really need to know this, not because I am obsessed with statistics or really enjoy the word 'benchmarking', or because I want to feed an obsessive statistical bureaucracy, but because it helps me to assess, differentiate, personalise and adjust my content and delivery. It gives my reflections meaning and allows me to direct appropriate support to where it is needed. If I can take what I have to do – NC, levels, targets, benchmarks, syllabus, tests, value added, etc. – and make it human I can hold true to what I believe is good teaching while also satisfying the needs of those to whom I am increasingly accountable.

Creating a classroom climate for successful assessment

What this chapter will explore:

- How successful classroom assessment depends on the right classroom climate
- The correct physical, emotional and relational climate for successful classroom assessment
- How to exploit your model as a successful learner and teacher

'I am terribly afraid of falling myself', said the Cowardly Lion, *'but I suppose there is nothing to do but try it.'*

(L. Frank Baum, *Wizard of Oz*)

Productive classroom assessment thrives in classrooms that are safe, stimulating and owned. It is led by passionate teachers who are willing to take risks. It is also led by students who are engaged, autonomous and responsible for their own learning and assessment. It starts with the right classroom climate, the roots of the tree, providing a stable base for introducing new strategies and ways of assessing. Strong branches are represented by new skills, attitudes and behaviours in autonomous assessment, meta-cognition, respecting boundaries, peer assessment, negotiated target setting, differentiation and personalisation, and managing active assessment. As you develop the work the processes embed into the life of the classroom and intertwine thinking, learning and assessing. The fruit that the tree bears is learners who can learn, assess, guide, question and reflect for themselves. Learners who can confidently meet challenges without fear of failure. As students mature and move through education and employment it is these skills that are critical to achieving success.

For assessment to be effective a safe emotional environment within the classroom is essential. A classroom climate where the teacher's voice is dominant is not a place for truly reflective assessment. For conversations about learning to thrive, the emotional environment must be safe enough for everyone to take a risk. Any procedures that you introduce for classroom assessment will be constantly undermined if the climate and rapport between students and teacher and between the students themselves is not productive. Successful assessment depends not just on the process or system that you choose to employ with your students. Your insistence on assessing what is working first and examining what is not second should be a deliberate ploy. It protects and develops fragile self-esteem, breaks down limiting self-belief and establishes an infectious example for the group to follow.

Creating the right environment for successful assessment means addressing the relational physical and emotional climate in your classroom.

Relationships and rapport

(This section on relationships and rapport is taken from *The Essential Guide to Taking Care of Behaviour*.)

Building a lasting professional relationship that meets the needs of both teacher and student is a balancing act that requires the skill and experience of a high-wire act. Any fool can befriend a student at the expense of their own dignity – 'Call me Bob'; at the expense of other members of staff – 'I don't much like him either'; or at the expense of their own pocket – 'Take this golden iPod as a reward/gift/ bribe for your efforts'. A relationship that is based on a pseudo 'friendship' can jog along quite happily until the moment where the frustrations of learning need to be addressed, when deadlines must be kept and when confidence wobbles. Most of us accept our friends for what they are without attempting to draw the boundaries for them. In a learning environment, where boundaries must be drawn, friendship blurs the boundaries, sending mixed messages to your students.

Mutual trust and respect are earned not bestowed. It is not about trying to get 'down with the kids'. There are learning and behaviour boundaries that you expect your students to adhere to. So it goes with all teacher/student relationships.

Parent on the shoulder

'Parent on the shoulder' is a useful guide to check that your conversations with students are appropriate and the relationship a professional one. Imagine that, regardless of the context in which you are in, your conversations can be overheard by the student's parent. If you maintain this level of self-awareness you will not go far wrong. You will start to control your emotional responses when students frustrate you and be more aware of the boundaries that parents expect you to respect.

Some students do not understand why there must be such boundaries, some are just excited to get to know you better, whilst others deliberately try to overstep the mark and gain information in order to achieve an advantage. Revealing too much about your personal and social life may score some cool points, but can be easily misinterpreted and misreported. In an increasingly litigious society, where child protection is uppermost in the minds of parents, you do not want to risk being misinterpreted.

For some students you will need to define the boundaries and expectations of your professional relationship. This is particularly pertinent on trips and visits, where expectations can change as more of your personal routines are revealed. In a digital context, where more private communication is the norm, these boundaries may need to be drawn with a thicker line. MySpace, Bebo and Facebook are for friends, not for teachers and current students.

Building mutual trust with students is not just a core responsibility of the teacher but is the foundation for the fourth R, Rapport. Seasoned professionals know that the key is to be friendly but not friends, to be honest but not reveal personal lives, and to be open but not transparent.

The emotional climate

Your model often has the most impact on the behaviour and attitudes of the students you teach. 'Sit down, shut up and do your peer assessment' is unlikely to result in a productive assessment conversation. Neither of course is 'Danny why don't you take Claire's work to mark and try to forget that she stabbed you with a compass yesterday'.

It starts with your own behaviour. You set the climate for your classroom in both behaviour and learning.

There are some classrooms where failure is equated with fear and shame and others where there is an honesty about failure being part of learning. There are some classrooms where students are openly laughed at for their mistakes and others that are more forgiving of experimentation and failure. There are some classrooms where humans are expected to be perfect and others where fallibility is accepted.

Assessment has an emotional impact. It is easy to assess; the skill is to engage the participants in the assessment process so that they are willing to listen to a criticism, to act on targets and to engage in a reflective process without fear or embarrassment. To create a classroom where participants have ownership, investment and a reason to engage. To create a climate in the classroom where discussions are not tinged with competition, jealousy, resentment or revenge for some minor misdemeanour. All this is achievable. It takes time, effort, clear boundaries and some clear modelling.

Teacher as learner: your model

There is an advertising campaign at the moment in Australia showing parents smoking, arguing with other drivers, dropping litter, etc. as their children follow them doing exactly the same thing. The message is hard-hitting but simple: 'children see, children do'. In the classroom there are many influences on the way that students learn and behave. We already appreciate that our behaviour has a direct effect on the way that those around us behave; perhaps it is time to transfer the same idea to teaching and learning.

The teacher's most effective model is one that is rarely demonstrated: the role of the learner. Teachers are successful learners who have taken risks in learning, experienced periods of intensive study, taken stressful examinations, and felt success, failure and rejection. Their resilience as learners is a model to aspire to. Teachers know how to succeed when what they are being asked to do is outside their comfort zone. Yet how many of us learn something new in front of or with the class? When do we demonstrate our skills as autonomous learners? How do we show our use of goal-setting, reflective self-assessment, action planning, etc.? How often do we have open and honest discussions about the process of learning that includes aspects of our own learning that we still struggle with? If your students only ever see you being successful, getting it right and knowing the answer, then the model for them is unrealistic. By not being honest about failure we can unwittingly establish a model that your students can not understand. Some of them will experience failure every day and may begin to fear that they might be the only ones who do so.

The expectation of perfection is asking too much. I like students to see me struggle to learn something or experience frustration with a task, and to help me map what I have learned and reflect on the next steps. It marks me out as a learner, creates a sense of equality, and demystifies the skills and steps in learning, resilience and higher-order thinking.

> **TOP TIP!**
>
> *Display learning maps or learning journeys on the wall with students reinforcing their own work and the work of others by adding to them daily. For younger children, use trees with golden leaves and have leaf ceremonies at the end of the day, and peer assessment leaves. For older students, use road maps with route planners between grades or ladders of competence with new targets for each new rung.*

The constructive emotional climate

For assessment to motivate, encourage, sustain interest and engage it must be a process that searches for what is right, what has been done well and what was successful in the first instance. Assessment that merely identifies what is not right is a shortcut that demotivates, reinforces limited self-belief and teaches students to reflect primarily on what is going badly. All of which are lessons that they may well carry for the rest of their lives.

It is certainly easier, quicker and less effort to deconstruct and identify what is wrong. Effective teaching, however, rarely relies on quick and easy shortcuts. For students who have a difficult history in education, who have grown used to failing assessments or who have failed without ever really understanding why, the constant search for what is wrong has a long-term impact. Few people thrive in an environment where assessment conversations search for fault. Many find themselves conditioned to search for the same in others. The long-term fallout can be seen all around us in the adult world. Emotionally intelligent assessment, on the other hand, is the relentless search for the cup that is half full.

It is simple rituals that embed positive reinforcement in the process, that force over-critical students to reflect on the positive in peer assessment and build mutual trust within the group. It is this classroom climate that makes difficult conversations smoother and unwelcome news easier to deliver.

Finding fault in the work of others is in our DNA. It is not a skill that needs to be taught or, indeed, encouraged. I am not sure if it is something that is a universal part of the human condition, or if it is connected with 'Britishness' or living on an island, but the ability to look at something and immediately find fault with it is within all of us. At times this is where we find our humour, our common ground, our camaraderie. Often it is playful, almost harmless. In some situations it is expected and even accepted. In teaching and learning it plays havoc with the classroom atmosphere, expectations, relationships, self-esteem and achievement. It heightens students' attention to the errors and neglects to reinforce what has been achieved. Just as students begin to understand a concept/idea/language they can be peppered with criticism. The growth of new learning is easily stunted.

The audience who watch a play just waiting for a line to be dropped might easily miss the most beautiful soliloquy. The child who lives with criticism learns to condemn.

> '*I have missed more than 9,000 shots in my career. I have lost almost 300 games. On 26 occasions I have been entrusted to take the game winning shot … and I missed. I have failed over and over and over again in my life. And that's precisely why I succeed.*'

> (Michael Jordan)

Classrooms that seek to encourage and to balance feedback are safe, nurturing places in which to learn.

Why not try this?

3:1

Before anyone is allowed to criticise the work of someone else (including the teacher!) they must first find three aspects of the work that are good. Insist on it, model it overtly and make it central to your classroom assessment. Apply it to yourself and to your students, when you are marking work, talking to students about their work, asking for feedback in class, drawing together ideas at the end of the lesson, discussing students with colleagues, talking to parents/mentors/tutors, structuring targets, writing comments on reports or teaching new behaviours.

This way you can change the habits of lazy learners and reverse the seemingly inbuilt ability of everyone to look for fault first. The 3:1 rule can be quickly adopted and will become a classroom ritual that everyone recognises the value of.

Assessment is personal. It is covered in layers of emotion, self-doubt, arrogance, fear and excitement. Yet we want students to be able to reflect on their work without seeing a poor reflection of themselves. Say the spelling in a piece of work is poor. This does not mean that the student can not spell or, at worst, they are stupid. It means that today, in this piece of work, the student has some adjustments to make. Similarly, a student's poem is level 7, sensitive and intelligent. This does not mean that we should be recommending him or her as Poet Laureate. By separating students' identity from their achievement or failure we can protect self-esteem through assessment processes, be they gentle, rigorous or exacting.

Risk is essential

Being able to take a risk distinguishes a good classroom climate. Classrooms where students feel they can take a risk without fear of ridicule, embarrassment or shame are classrooms where students learn faster and are in greater control of their learning. Imagine learning a foreign language without ever taking the risk to speak it aloud, trying to comprehend particle physics without discussing it or learning to ride a bike without getting on one. Risk in wider society has negative connotations: financial risks, health risks, health and safety risks. In the classroom it is an essential element of successful formative assessment. Risk-taking when you are just learning a new skill or concept is, as they say, 'a big ask'. It needs a great deal of trust between peers and confidence in the teacher. Yet classrooms where risks are taken are fascinating places in which to learn. They are filled with the excitement of new ideas, the honesty of how humans learn, unexpected turns, and a common pursuit of understanding.

Strategy spotlight

Simple ways to encourage students to take a risk when answering questions

'There are only two places in the world where time takes precedence over the job to be done. School and prison.'

(William Glasser)

The competitive nature of many human beings means that many of us are not given time to think. The urgency of many lessons – 'I have got to finish this unit/module/scheme or they won't be ready for ... ' and the pressures of delivering a set curriculum leads many teachers into bad habits. Instead of modelling patience by waiting the extra few seconds it takes for a student to formulate an answer, it is tempting to move onto another student who might provide a more speedy response. Try saying 'Take your time, try and take a risk by speaking your thoughts aloud, you know that I don't always say the right thing first time' and making your model clear.

Being patient and quelling the fear of anyone who feels uncomfortable speaking out in front of their peers is an excellent model for all of your students to follow. The idea that we can formulate perfect answers every time is an unrealistic and damaging expectation.

Set the right model and tone: 'Thank you for taking a risk by speaking your thoughts aloud.' Give students time to construct their ideas – the extra five seconds are so often well worth the waiting. Experiment with other mechanisms for students to show they have the answer (see box). 'Hands up' often means that one student's declaration that they have the answer stops everyone else from thinking.

Why not try this?

Some mechanisms for students to show they have the answer:

- Say 'Look at me when you have the answer and look away if you are still thinking'.

- Individual dry wipe boards held up to the class or to a partner after some thinking time. (Once the minority have got over the excitement of drawing large willies on their boards this can work well!)

- Sticky notes to collate everyone's thoughts that are placed in groups or brought to the front and stuck on a post, wall or flipchart.

- Subtle indicators on desks so that you can guage each student's confidence with their answer as you tour the room. Many teachers use traffic lights, smiley faces or thumbs up/down. Try asking the students to make a simple 1–10 slider, which is then placed discreetly on each desk. Pose the question and ask students to place the pointer on the appropriate number once they have their answer. Clearly your 1–10 scale can be adapted for all sorts of subtle communication with the teacher, such as: 'How motivated do you feel?', 'How urgent is your request for help?', 'How much of this do you understand?', 'How good will you feel when you have understood it?', 'How good was you weekend?'

- Ask older students to send the answer by Bluetooth from their mobile phones.

- Remember to reward those who get the answer right and those who have taken a thoughtful risk, not with sweets and presents but with a smile and sincere positive reinforcement.

- Try giving everyone time to think and then using a random name selector. You can draw names from a hat or set this up on PowerPoint by entering each student's name on a separate slide and then setting the transition timings to their fastest setting so that the slideshow scrolls through quickly. When you click the mouse or keyboard the slide will stop on a random name.

The physical environment for successful assessment

Most displays celebrate work that has been completed. For many, display is the culmination of a project or activity. A recognition that the work has been success-ful and has resulted in outcomes that everyone is proud of. There is certainly room for display that celebrates, but it does not need to be the dominant theme. In fact, in surveys with over 4000 students at secondary and further education (FE) level on students' attitudes towards classroom display I found that at least 50 per cent of students did not want their work on display. Reasons varied from fear of ridicule, to not believing that the work is worthy, to thinking it would be damaged.

There is much more we can do to use display to promote assessment skills and autonomous attitudes. Teachers who design displays that reflect more than just the outcome know that the display can also be a reflection of the process and direction of learning. Moreover, it can lead students' understanding of the success criteria, of the quality of work needed to achieve a certain grade and encourage them to consider their next steps.

If we consider displays as an aid for learning and assessment, then if what they display changes daily, it is far more transient and probably a bit messier, but is much more relevant to the work that the students are currently undertaking.

A classroom that gears its display to support assessment might have the following:

- Key words, wow words (devilishly tricky extended vocabulary that you can impress other people with) and key terminology with spaces for students to note definitions and explanations.

- Diagrams and ideas – mind maps, drafts and sketches, spider diagrams and maps of learning.

- Photographs of 'eureka' and 'a-ha' moments.

- Assessment criteria matched to examples of work, blown up on large sheets and connected with pins and string or coloured wool or large markers.

- Target records for each group or student as lists, bookmarks, graphs and mobiles.

- Lists of agreed and negotiated criteria with students' names, stickers or smilies beside them.

- Clear boundaries and routines established for peer, self- and group assessment as text or as a set of icons that are agreed and easily read.

There is room for completed work outside the classroom, in the corridors, scroll-ing on the screen, loaded onto digital photo frames, on the intranet or in the reception area. If you find that you don't have enough room then consider taking down all those pre-printed 'motivational' posters that seem worthy but really have no impact on success at all. If you move between teaching spaces then digital photo frames are great for scrolling though the examples that you want on show or carry large art folders that can stand on the desk.

In many FE colleges and some secondary schools display is minor importance outside an OFSTED inspection. Most recognise the value of display, of working in an environment that is clearly focused on learning and achievement, but few see that they have the time to sustain a high-quality display. Take the same teachers into a busy primary classroom and they are immediately struck by the quality of display, the cacophony of ideas and the vibrancy of the colours. The best classrooms have so much display of work in progress that there is little room on the walls for anything else. The windows are splattered with maps of ideas, the back of the door holds a rolling record of key terminology and from the ceiling hang prompts for questioning and feedback. The room is less like a manicured classroom and more like a lunatic's laboratory. Through the apparent chaos of ideas students habitually make their sense and sense their control over what and how they are learning.

Reflecting on practice

As a slightly nervous and apprehensive visitor I sat in the reception area trying to gauge the school and weigh up how the day ahead might go. The portents were not good: an abundance of hair accessories, trainers, swearing, a whiff of cigarette smoke and a tide of teenagers wafting past. The carpets were just held together with a mass of chewing gum, the environment was graffiti-stained and bleak, and showed no evidence of display. Anxious staff scurried in and rumours bounced around that a priest had been attacked on the estate the night before. I braced myself.

Working with the English department was not easy. I sat through a chaos of lessons in which teachers struggled to maintain control, and between the inevitable 'What the f*** are you doing here?' conversations with the delightful students in the back row I pondered the bleak state of the room. Old displays hung their heads in shame and wept. It made a 'Grange Hill' classroom look cared for. In the corridors displays had become victims of the scrawling of marauding teenagers, pushing and tearing. They reflected a lack pride, of self-esteem and ownership. I resolved to tackle it immediately.

Over the next two days we set to work on the corridors, and tried to counter the inevitable defeatism of passing teachers. Yet as we worked and those who passed sensed our determination and enthusiasm for the task, students offered their help. At the end of the day five students stayed behind to help, and by lunchtime the next day we were turning them away. In two days the corridors were transformed by the hard work of some unlikely students.

→

Staff and students alike began stopping and appreciating the work. The students who had helped were motivated to do more and so with a box of resources they set about transforming other corridors, with other departments queuing up for help. The 'Display Team' was born and teachers realised that being surrounded by great display didn't necessarily cost them time or effort.

Returning two weeks later I was curious to see what state the new displays were in. There were some curling corners certainly, but on the whole the displays were undamaged, respected and, with passing students saying 'That was my idea', they were most certainly owned.

Practical strategies specific to primary, secondary and post-16

Primary

Subtle communication

Subtle communication between the student and the teacher makes it easier to judge when to intervene and when to leave the student to work independently. Try mechanisms for instant feedback, e.g. traffic light symbols: red for 'Help!', amber for 'I am getting on but have a question' and green for 'Leave me alone, I am flying'.

Learn something new alongside your students

Let them see you learn and misunderstand, succeed and, most importantly, fail. Choose a topic that is as challenging for you as it is for the students – learning to juggle, designing a collage, building structures from straws.

Use images, icons and photographs

Not just for those who are learning to read but for everyone. Ritualise assessment procedures and nurture understanding of the same.

Secondary

First 5

As the turmoil of the teenage years overtakes the excitement of learning in many students you have to work harder to sustain an appropriate classroom climate. The first five minutes of the lesson are critical. Stand at the door and welcome your students with a handshake and a smile, be pleased to see them even when you are not. As you set the expectations for the lesson high, infect them with your overwhelming enthusiasm, determination and passion for your subject. Match your performance with content that is intriguing, inclusive and involving.

Seating plans

Retain control over the seating plan, who works with who and boys working with girls. Challenge the friendship group, tribe and gang divides that emerge in teenworld by constantly changing the mix of students and insisting on all students learning and assessing together.

Play together

Simple games quickly build trust and relationships. Try 'Counting to 20'. Place an object for everyone to stare at in the middle of a circle of students. The aim of the game is to count up to 20 in order, but students must not look at each other or plan a strategy. If two people speak at the same time then the game starts again. As well as showing your students that we listen with our eyes, you will gently encourage risk and team work, and sow the seeds of mutual trust and respect.

Post-16

Treating students as adults

As students want to be treated like adults define what this means with them. What are the rights and responsibilities of the adult world? How do adults learn together? What are the accepted rituals, routines and manners of a professional working environment? Spend time on it with them and do not assume that they already know even the most common learning behaviours.

Student teaching

Regularly ask students to teach lessons or segments of the lesson. Have a rolling rota with a regular slot planned. Demand that students take responsibility for learning and support them discreetly as they do so.

Securing relationships

Seek to proactively develop positive relationships with those students who keep under the radar as well as those who you can not miss. Some students will have developed advanced rituals to avoid speaking out in front of the class, answer questions or interact with other people. Find time to gently build the relationship: say 'hello' whenever you see them around the site; share a book, film or idea that you think might interest them; privately reinforce their contributions to classwork; use teachers they already have a strong relationship with to pass on positive messages; spend a moment writing a more personal and reflective comment at the end of marked work; find time for informal conversation. The students' trust in you is critical to them being able to take a risk.

Exercise

Try these true or false questions for yourself. You might like to give them to the students as a catalyst for discussions around the new strategies that you are considering.

	True	False
Students over the age of 11 know how to work independently		
How the teacher learns affects the way that students learn		
How people learn is scientifically proven		
Setting targets for other people is a waste of time		
A grade is all that is needed to mark students' work		
It is not the teacher's responsibility to teach students *how* to learn		
There is no place for rote learning in modern teaching		
Three-part lessons improve learning		
It is up to students to decide if they are going to learn		
Teachers and students can be true friends		
'You can learn more about someone in an hour of play than in a year of conversation'		

Critical questions

- How do you use goal setting, action plans, target setting and reflective self-assessment in your own learning?
- How can you share this with your students?
- When do you plan to learn with and in front of your students?
- How could you give your students responsibility for display?

Conclusion

Without the right classroom climate there is no point introducing strategies to give the students ownership. Responsibility for assessment can not usefully be passed over to students who are trying to work in an adversarial environment. The resilience, empathy and kindness of your students is the difference between students who work with each other and those that help each other to learn. By directly addressing the classroom climate you are investing time that you will recoup through genuinely productive peer, self-, teacher and group assessment.

Key ideas summary

- Insist on assessing what is working first and examining what is not second.

- 'Children see, children do' – your model as a learner is critical, you are an expert in failure as well as success.

- Assessment has an emotional impact, classroom assessment breaks down in classrooms where the climate is not safe to take risks and accept honest criticism.

- 3:1 – identifying three positive aspects of the work earns the right to offer a criticism.

- Encourage risk taking in learning, in yourself and in your students.

- Make the boundaries of mutual trust and respect clear and unassailable.

- Display the quality of a good primary school, leave no space uncovered, use the displays to support current work and leave the retrospectives for the corridors.

Going further

Medina, J. (2008) *Brain Rules*, Pear Press.

The National Association for Prevention of Child Abuse and Neglect, 'Children see, children do' campaign: www.napcan.org.au/index.htm

How far have we come?

The assessment tree

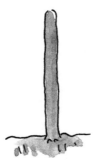

The foundation for productive classroom assessment is developing. The emotionally secure classroom gives other strategies a firm base and stability. With roots spreading, new growth is inevitable. Students feel confident in taking a risk.

Autonomous assessment, motivated learners

- How to successfully nurture responsibility for assessment for and with your students
- How teaching skills and rituals in self-reflection, time management and thinking create confident autonomous learners
- How formulaic approaches to learning restrict autonomy and encourage 'spoon-feeding'

'We cannot have real learning in school if we think it is our duty and our right to tell children what they must learn.'

(John Holt, 1990)

Autonomous learners take responsibility for their assessment, not by chance but by design. They have been taught the skills that enable them to assess and differentiate independently. Empowering students to take responsibility for their own learning and assessment does not mean simply cutting them adrift. Nurturing autonomy with frameworks that provide support means that you spend less time 'spoon-feeding' students and more time with them discussing learning. Motivating students to take control of their own assessment is a cultural shift for most classrooms. Promoting and embedding autonomous learning can lead to a huge change in the quality of assessment in the classroom.

Autonomy and nurturing independent learning

At some point we have to recognise that personalised learning is unattainable while the teacher remains in control of the learning. The model of education that we have is far from perfect, but with some simple alterations to our daily routines we can create the conditions for autonomous learning to be taught and for classroom assessment to thrive.

When we have autonomy in our working lives we are empowered, motivated and feel in control of decision making. When we have orders that are imposed from above, or restrictive syllabi that tell us how to teach, it is tempting to become demotivated, to feel powerless and to respond with subversion or cynicism. In the workplace autonomy is central to our motivation. It is the same with students.

Teaching to tests, exams and external criteria does not foster autonomy. The culture of unnecessary testing works against the autonomy that we want to promote. It stifles the curriculum, restricts true differentiation, puts even young children off learning and serves only those with a fetish for tickboxes. With teachers under increasing pressure to deliver more content, more quickly, it seems that giving students greater responsibility will only slow up the assessment process. In practice the initial investment of time pays off many times over.

It is possible to jump through the hoops of testing with some flair – to make what we have to do human. We can help students to become genuinely autonomous learners within an imperfect system. With skilful teaching we can work within the limitations to create classrooms where students are keen to accept responsibility and take more control for themselves.

Classrooms where teachers teach and students listen are not autonomous; classrooms where the teacher 'knows everything' are rarely so. For teachers it is partly a question of skills and partly a willingness to take a risk and ring the changes.

Responsibility

Giving students responsibility for seemingly frivolous tasks is the first step towards emphasising autonomy in your classroom. Teachers who only give students responsibility for 'sitting down and shutting up' wonder why they won't take responsibility for their own learning, for deadlines and for themselves. In primary school classrooms there is a great deal of autonomy in learning and organisation. It could be argued that in primary education we already teach children to be autonomous: 'You all need to fetch your equipment from the boxes, everyone has a responsibility for tidying up'; 'Joel can you lead the group discussion?' In secondary education, however, autonomy can be seen as a threat or an unnecessary risk: 'Right, I am giving out the scissors, don't touch them until you are told to, stay in your seat unless you have written permission, sit down, shut up and learn!'

Why not try this?

Simple tasks that students are given responsibility for save you time, encourage their independence and set a more collaborative tone.

Which tasks are you doing for the students that they are perfectly capable of doing for themselves? From handing out equipment, to preparing the room, to putting up and maintaining displays, how much responsibility can you give? Who is responsible for organising learning? How can you invite and allocate responsibility?

Let's start with purely organisational tasks. Use the charts below to audit how much responsibility rests with the adults and how much with the students in your classroom.

Task	Teacher	LSA – other	Students
Handing out and organising equipment			
Preparing the room for the lesson			
Designing and creating displays (consider using a team of students)			
Maintaining displays in the classroom			
Tidying the room at the end of the lesson			
Negotiating rules and expectations			
Making decisions on time needed for tasks			
Reminding other students about the agreed conduct – turning off phones, etc.			➡

Task	Teacher	LSA – other	Students
Ordering resources and equipment			
Organising store cupboards			
Collecting homework and chasing late work			
Moving furniture for different configurations			

Then, taking responsibility for learning ...

Task	Teacher	LSA – other	Students
Creating a starter activity			
Contributing ideas for extension tasks			
Deciding on groupings			
Teaching other students specific concepts and skills			
Leading sections of the lesson			
Negotiating deadlines for homework and coursework			
Recording targets			
Designing personal and class learning blogs			
Maintaining a learning blog for the group			
Organising study and support groups			
Leading the plenary			
Feeding back to the teacher regarding the quality of teaching			

As ever your model is critical here. We are all human, yet it is important that our personal disorganisation and fallibility does not prove to be a poor model for our students.

If you hold onto all of the responsibility then don't be surprised when your students find it difficult to take even the first steps towards autonomous learning. Rather than creating a revolution tomorrow by handing over your schemes of work to your students, make a plan to gradually delegate more responsibility. Start with simple tasks and take a risk with students who might not seem able to accept responsibility. Let them feel that they are trusted, that they can take more ownership. Be prepared for them to respond fantastically, while resolving to be persistent with students who try to reject the idea that they need to get more involved.

'It's my time that you are wasting!' – teaching time-management skills

Whose time is it really? Discussions surrounding time are often just clichés: 'It's your time you are wasting', 'You are wasting my time now', 'I'm waiting for you', and so on, and so on. What is the correct emphasis for the responsibility for managing time?

> **TOP TIP!**
>
> *As part of your daily habits when starting students on a task, resist imposing a deadline and instead ask them how much time they think they need to do it. As students become practised in predicting, negotiating and working to deadlines your lessons will start to run like clockwork.*

We all have had lessons that ran over or fell short, lessons where we lost track of time because we were so involved in an activity, and occasions where we set more homework because we ran out of time. Perhaps it may be better to share the responsibility for managing time with the students.

It is not unusual to hear teachers who have set long, unsupported deadlines for major pieces of coursework complaining bitterly that work is very slow in coming in and is of poor quality. They are often working with students who have little experience of taking responsibility for their own learning and managing and organising their own time. At the opposite end of the scale there are students who appear to be spoon-fed, who are given an unfair amount of leniency with deadlines and who lean far too much on their teacher.

When adults find it difficult to manage their own time they soon discover structures through which they can prioritise their work. The same ideas can be taught, understood and used by students: Stephen Covey's time-management quadrants (see Figure 2.1) can be useful for older students (Covey, 1989). The same terminology can be embedded in classroom teaching and used to support students as they learn how to manage their own time. The responsibility for time management can not be the teacher's responsibility. Students can be taught how to take responsibility.

Covey's quadrants

Quadrant 1 **Urgent and important**	Quadrant 2 **Important but not urgent**
'Firefighting: the activities need to be dealt with immediately and they are important'	'Quality time: important to your long-term goals but can be scheduled in'
Teacher: reports to be handed in by 9 am, the computer has blown up, Darren is damp	Mentoring individual students, redesigning a scheme of work, having a social life
Quadrant 3 **Urgent but not important**	Quadrant 4 **Neither urgent nor important**
'Distractions that need to be dealt with immediately but are not really important'	'Time wasting'
Witney's question about the trip, the phone call from the supplier, the text you just got	Meetings that last longer than 45 minutes, writing targets for students, predicting grades 18 months before the exam

Figure 2.1: How Covey's quadrants relate to your *own* time management

Source: Adapted from Covey, S.R. (1989) *The 7 Habits of Highly Effective People*, Simon and Schuster. Reproduced with permission

Use the quadrants with students to:

- Help students plan intensive periods of self-study. Ask them to list everything that they have to do before an examination. Include activities that are personal as well as work related. Pair up students and ask them to place the activities where they think that they ought to go. Use this map as a starting point for discussion with peers and for negotiation with the teacher.

- Focus attention on how students are spending their time in lessons. Ask them to observe and list them. Include work-related tasks as well as social activities, pencil sharpening, issuing mild threats, etc.

- Share with students how you prioritise your own time. Model use of the quadrants by demonstrating how you guide yourself through periods of intensive work.

- Negotiate realistic deadlines for homework and staged deadlines for coursework: 'I need this coursework in four weeks. How will you share this time between the first, second and third quadrants' 'When do you expect that this coursework will move into the red quadrant?'.

- Plan larger projects alongside students.

- Refer to in conversation, for example 'Carl you are drifting into the fourth quadrant'.

Student voice

Teaching students to be autonomous decision makers means affording them a voice over how they are taught. Students' opinions on the quality of their teachers are already well established on the internet. From covert recordings in lessons, to www.RateMyTeacher.com to Friends Reunited and Facebook-style networks, your students are already able to publicly assess the quality of your teaching, anonymously and without any fear of reprisal. Why not harness their enthusiasm, give them an opportunity to do it that keeps the feedback private, and design processes that are useful to teachers and students alike.

'We are ushering in a new world of accountability in which parents, patients and local communities shape the services they receive, ensuring all our public services respond not simply to the hand of government, but to the voice of local people … People take it for granted that they will access other people's reviews and ratings before buying something on eBay or Amazon, and yet we do not yet have systematic access to other people's experiences when choosing a GP practice or nursery. We have clearly got the balance wrong when online businesses have higher standards of transparency than the public services we pay for and support.'

(Gordon Brown, 2009)

Before everyone else finds out about how your students feel about your teaching you might want to hear the feedback. It is bound to be useful and, other than from a small minority, is usually more balanced and fair than your own assessment of yourself. To do this takes a leap of faith and is a risk. Yet effective learning requires risk taking in adults in the same way that it does in students.

Let your students hold up the mirror for you

Ask students to assess your teaching. Invite regular critiques using the same assessment methods that are used to assess their work.

TOP TIP!

Try giving each student a voting slip or chip at the end of the lesson and ask them to drop it into one of three pots marked 'Perfectly paced', 'A little too fast for me' or 'Not fast enough' or 'Great lesson, thank you', 'Ok' or 'Must try harder'. For younger children translate the text into images, faces or photographs to ensure that everyone can have their say.

Students can also give useful feedback by grading the suitability of homework on an agreed scale and writing this mark at the bottom of their work, e.g. 'On a scale of 1–5 how hard/interesting/engaging/useful was this homework?' Many institutions have trained students to observe lessons in a more formal style. They use simple questions that are student-focused to help reflect rather than judge the teacher. An example of a student observation sheet is given below.

Example of a student observation sheet

Teacher talk time (How much time does the teacher talk to the whole class?)	How many positive comments does the teacher use? Make a tally	How many negative comments does the teacher use? Make a tally	How much did the students enjoy the lesson? Circle one	How much did the teacher enjoy the lesson? Circle one
	+	-	1 2 3 4 5 6 7 8 9 10	1 2 3 4 5 6 7 8 9 10

Plot how motivated you feel on this graph every 5 minutes:

```
10
 9
 8
 7
 6
 5
 4
 3
 2
 1
 0   5   10   15   20   25   30   35   40   45   50   55   60
```

→

Example of a student observation sheet *continued*

Write any questions that you have for the teacher here

List three things that you found interesting in the lesson:

1

2

3

Give one aspect of the teaching that you think needs work:

Institutions that value the voice of the students reinforce the autonomy that you are building with your students in the classroom. Collecting student opinion to reinforce decisions that are already being made by the adults is not affording students a real voice. The key question is 'Why are we asking students for their opinion?' When you have an answer to this then there are some more ideas for the next question: 'How do we do it?'

Different ways to gain student opinion

- Student Learning Consultants
- Student councils
- Peer mentoring
- On-the-spot interviews

- Diary room for students to air their views
- Community or faculty council
- Student associate governors
- Student surgeries
- Rate my teacher using the VLE (Virtual learning platform)
- Student design consultants for liaising with new building and maintenance projects
- Student surveys and questionnaires
- Student interview panels

Self-reflection

'Self assessment far from being a luxury is in fact an essential component of formative assessment'.

(Paul Black and Dylan Wiliam, 1998)

Autonomous learners assess their own performance and have been taught to do so. For successful classroom assessment to be sustained, students need to be taught the skills of productive self-reflection and how to avoid the pitfalls of consistently reflecting on the negative aspects of their work.

Teaching self-reflection demands more emphasis than a quick 'think about what you have done' prompt. Encouraging and at times requiring students to spend time reflecting on their own understanding/performance/achievement/failure is teaching them the skills that successful learners employ every day.

Introspection is Howard Gardner's **intra**personal intelligence (Gardner, 1993). People who have developed strong intrapersonal intelligence have a good sense of self and their own abilities as a learner. Assessing with students who constantly rely on the opinions of the teacher and other students to gauge their own progress is a one-way process. If education prepares students for the adult world then they must learn to rely on themselves, on their own assessment of their progress, and they need to have established rituals that produce honest, rational and reflective thoughts. Leave your students dependent on your approval and they may not find a replacement in the working world. It is not safe to rely on employers to offer regular balanced reflections on performance.

Many students learn their skills of self-reflection through prayer. Yet there are many who have not practised ritualised self-reflection, some whose home lives prevent it, and many more who are working so hard and at such a pace that they feel they have no time for it.

A ritual that can be taught to students of all ages is Naikan Self-reflection, or the Japanese Art of Self Reflection (Krech, 2002). Using simple questions you can begin practising and encouraging self-reflection with and alongside your students.

Ask the students to reflect and make private lists from three questions: 'What did you receive from others today?', 'What did you give to others today?', 'What troubles and difficulties did you cause others today?' It is important to be specific rather than general. For example, rather than state that you received food today, write down the actual food that you received and ate today. Don't leave items off your list because they seem 'trivial' or you receive them everyday; it is quite important to notice and list just such items.

Balanced self-reflection is at the heart of good mental health. Our habits in self-reflection do not always lead us to productive reflections. Some consider their own efforts and achievements too highly, others habitually concentrate on what has gone wrong. Simple structures work well, are remembered easily and teach better habits. You can ask the students to relate the three questions to a subject, a relationship or a context:

- What have I received from my teacher/learning French/my time at college?
- What have I given to my teacher/the modern languages department/the college?
- What troubles and difficulties have I caused my teacher/other students/the college staff?

Coloured thinking hats

Another practical application of self-reflective prompts can be seen in de Bono's coloured thinking hats (de Bono, 1985). The hats represent six modes of thinking and are a useful way to encourage students to independently examine their performance or an idea from all angles.

Red hat

This covers intuition, feelings and emotions, and requires no justification. The feeling may be genuine and the logic spurious! It gives the thinker permission to put forward his or her feelings on the subject at the moment: *'How do I feel about this right now?'*

Yellow hat

This is the logical and positive hat. It can be used in looking forward to the result of some proposed action or finding something of value in what has already happened: *'Why will this work and how will it offer benefits?'*

Black hat

Black hat thinking is logical; the hat of judgement and caution: *'Why does the suggestion not fit the facts/available experience/the system in use/the policy that is being followed?'*

Green hat

This is the hat of creativity, alternatives, proposals, different and new ideas, provocation and 'outside the box' thinking: *'How can this idea be modified to improve it?' 'What different ways can achieve the same objective?'*

White hat

Covers facts, figures, information needs and gaps: *'What information do we have, what do we need and where can we get it?' 'Let's drop the arguments and proposals and look at the database!'*

Blue hat

This is the overview or process control hat. It looks not at the subject itself but at the thinking about the question (metacognition): *'How have we been thinking so far and what types of thinking should we do more of?'*

Why not try this?

- Music played for two-minute reflective bursts to give students time for personal self-reflection.

- Directed self-reflection: bullet point three things you have done well and one that you need to work on, or say 'Be ready to tell your partner one idea you have had from your two minutes of self-reflection'.

- Creating images or diagrams that reflect on how the work is progressing. Individually on sticky notes or in an image diary, or with a huge roll of paper and all students surrounding it with marker pens.

- Suggesting different contexts: prepare a self-evaluation to give to a prospective employer or to show to your grandparent.

Strategy spotlight

Answer that question

We can take autonomy away from students by habitually trying to solve their problems, to proffer advice when it is not invited and by trying to think for them. There are some questions that need an answer and many that need another question.

Most of us have experience of working one-to-one with a student and finding ourselves answering questions that in hindsight they ought to have tackled themselves. Filling in gaps in their understanding feels like a useful shortcut at the time but can encourage an unhealthy reliance on the teacher to solve problems rather than provide support. Finding the balance is difficult, particularly if your new 'friend' thinks that all the answers have just sat down beside him or her. If you find yourself drifting into a dynamic where you have become the one answering questions for the student it is time to pedal the other way.

The skills that you need are commonly found in what is now called 'coaching' (previously referred to as good teaching!). Make a point of countering relentless questioning by reflecting rather than giving advice. You are consciously developing the conversation to give responsibility back to your students:

Student comment	Teacher response
'My chart is rubbish, do it for me'	'What could you do to improve this first bit?'
'What do I put here?'	'Can you show me what you think?'
'Tell me the answer'	'I may need your help to get that far. Can you compare …?'
'Why do I have to do this?'	'Are you able to describe …?'
'I'm bored/tired/suffering executive stress. Can you do it for me?'	'What would happen if you put your ideas alongside mine?'
'I don't understand any of this'	'Can you show me an instance when …?'
'Can you read it for me?'	'Perhaps you can tell me the word that you recognise?'

What you are doing is encouraging metacognitive skills with and for the students. It is these skills which will, in time, help them to successfully manage the frustrations of learning for themselves and overcome them. At first you will need to provide the prompts, in time they will begin metacognitive questioning and rituals in their own heads. The art is to know when to hold up the mirror, when to provide directions and when to produce the cushions for the softest landings.

Reflecting on practice

The three-part lesson plan is not a formula for autonomous learning

The best lessons are not set in three parts and do not necessarily follow accepted thinking on how and when students learn. Intelligent teachers know that they can not control learning. They choose to focus on what they can control – how they teach. Good teachers reveal learning rather than predict it, have flexibility but a clear vision and never assume that anyone has learned anything.

Business presentation advice seems to have been bought in wholesale through the three-part lesson plan. The business mantra is: 'Tell your audience what you're about to tell them, tell them it, then ask them to repeat what you told them.' This might be a simple model for teaching but it is not an effective or even mildly exciting model for learning or assessing learning. It loosely translates into many classrooms as objectives, activities, plenary. Or, 'this is what I have to teach you, now you are going to learn, can you remember what I said I was trying to teach you?'

The three-part lesson plan appears to have been universally accepted as the only 'correct' way to structure a lesson. The lesson is started with the objectives posted on the board, the teacher reads them out, the students forget them, and we go on with the lesson. In the plenary students are reminded of the objectives as they scramble to relate their learning back to them. Amidst the muttering of, 'Oh, is that what we were doing?', 'What does she want us to say?' or 'We already knew that before the lesson!' is a general disinterest in objectives and lots of lip service to a process that is repeated ad nauseum – 'Today I learned, again, that teachers are interested in what they want to teach and not what I would like to learn'. Intelligent students can subvert the format by listening to the objectives, predicting the outcomes, cruising through the lesson and responding correctly to the questions at the end.

The system seems to have been created to force the hand of a tiny minority who are unable to give structure to their teaching. It is not designed to support the vast majority of teachers who are more than capable of doing so or the vast majority of students who do not need formulaic teaching in order to learn.

There was a time, let us never forget, when objectives were not always revealed at the beginning of the lesson. A time when we accepted that

→

learning took longer, when it was embedded over time and not in a single lesson. It is perfectly possible to learn fantastically well through learning that is revealed, investigated and discovered. Safely dropping students into the middle of an experience, surrounding a child with a beautiful poem, surprising them with practical science or confusing them with the conundrums of pure maths is what makes teaching impact on the confusing brain filing system of human beings. It also makes teaching a privilege. Without prediction, preparation, explanations, objectives, WALT, WILT and outcomes, learning will take place. Not at a predetermined rate or in the order that others prescribe, but it will happen. You may not be able to quantify it all and satisfy everyone who wants to meddle with your teaching but that makes it no less valuable, useful, enjoyable and productive. At what point do we take our ball and stop playing a game that we do not believe in? At least, when do we start protesting that the rules are not in the students' interests?

TOP TIP!

Change your focus – good teaching relies on the students telling you what they have learned and when they learned it. Forgo the plenary, PowerPoint, learning outcomes and 'what we have learned' rituals and spend the time you have gained on trying to understand who has learned and who needs help.

Students are excited by learning in many different forms. They are not interested in the three-part lesson plan. They are not stirred by objectives or excited by responding to the 'Today we learned ... ', questions. The constraints on teaching are not placed there in the best interests of the students or teachers but so that others can assess, rate, quantify, analyse and, most of all, inspect with a tickbox.

I once went to a meeting where we were asked to assess the quality of a school in prose. There were six inspectors around the table who instantly and unanimously protested that they couldn't assess the quality of a school without a sheet of tickboxes. I want to tell you that I was surprised; I wasn't. I want to tell you that I enlightened them; I couldn't. They knew what made a good school, but only when it was written next to a box. Anything else just wasn't relevant.

Teaching formulas that try to control learning by predicting what (and in which timescale) content will be learned does not produce autonomous students. It produces students who expect to be fed and teachers who serve it on a spoon. Try messing with the structure:

- Instead of posting your objectives ask children what they know, need to know, would be interested to know about the subject.

- Reveal your objectives at the end of the lesson – 'What do you think I was trying to teach you?' is a much more honest approach.

- Don't rely on the plenary, check understanding today, tomorrow and, as a test, in two months' time.

- Test and try all theories on learning, use what works, and beware of anyone who is peddling 'the complete solution'.

- Hook children into learning by appealing to their innate ability to learn through pattern – rhyme, song, repetition, revisiting prior learning.

- If the objectives are vital then ensure children refer to them throughout the lesson. Catch students who begin to understand concepts/attitudes/skills by awarding a tick/sticker/smiley face/giraffe stamp each time.

- Question formulas that are more focused on short-term recall in preference to long-term memory.

- Stop setting targets for other people; it is a waste of time. Invest time in negotiating targets with the children and foster personal autonomy and responsibility for learning.

Practical strategies for primary, secondary and further education

Primary

Daily mantras

Create and rehearse mantras for and with the class. Japanese Reiki uses: 'Just for today … Do not get angry, do not worry, be thankful, do your duties, be kind to others'.

Reflecting

Simple questions for younger students to use for self-reflection: 'What have I done, what do I need to do now, what else do I need?' or 'What worked? Why?', 'What didn't work? Why?', 'What does this situation remind you of?', 'How can I use this experience?', 'How does this experience relate to other situations I've been in? What can I learn for that situation?', 'Knowing what I know now, what would I do differently next time?'

Signs and symbols

Faces that prompt questions for themselves – (smiley face) something I am happy about, (worried face) something I am worried about, (quizzical face) something that I have forgotten to do, etc.

Responsibility

As well as giving responsibility for the organisation of the room and resources, consider ways that you can develop responsibility for learning. Are there times where students who have finished support those who are struggling? Are there opportunities for students to take the lead on designing the display, listing the success criteria, leading the feedback for other groups or leading the class discussion?

Secondary

Invest time

Take time to make your students responsible for their learning and assessment and it will pay off. Taking control of classroom assessment may initially seem like a faster way of getting results, but it leaves you with the problem of accurately assessing large groups of students that you may only see once or twice a week. Once your students have been trained to take the lead in assessing at the task level, you will spend more time enjoying teaching and less time pushing bits of paper or keyboard buttons. Shift the emphasis from personal organisation to the organisation of learning. Be determined in the face of those who would rather not accept responsibility or autonomy in learning. Rotate responsibilities.

Teach time management

Shift the responsibility back to the learner. Monitor their work plans and schedules and guide where necessary. Ensure each student keeps a diary (paper or digital) to record and plan. Map the critical deadlines and spend time mapping the consequences of missing it. Plan in checkpoints in the lead up to critical deadlines. In the classroom share responsibility for timekeeping and negotiating length of activities.

Refining work

Suggest rigorous frameworks for designing, drafting or refining work, try research, plan, draft, review, redraft, get feedback, finalise. Put up examples of work at the various stages alongside photographs of students engaged and mind maps of ideas.

Raise the expectation

Some teachers' idea of promoting autonomy is 'Go and research this on the internet'. Get your students involved in pursuing their own interests within the subject by guiding them to resources rather than leaving it to luck or skill with a search engine.

Group work

Agree and display prominently the negotiated routine for successful group work. Cut out the conversations about the weekend or the football or Chelsea's hairdo by drawing up clear boundaries with the students. Teach and reinforce the new agreements with positive reinforcement; catch them doing it well rather than waiting for students to step over the line. Do you want them to establish group roles, have one minute each to speak, pass the conch or each contribute to a giant ideas map?

Further education/post-16

Lesson bullets

In a digital format on the learning platform or as a simple diary entry or as a 'tweet' or text from a mobile phone ask students to record three simple bullet points from each lesson. This might take the form of questions, further ideas for investigation, elements of the work that are now well understood, etc. At the end of the month look back over the records and use them to map progression and celebrate achievement.

Homework and self study

Allow students to manage their own homework by offering choices. You might offer over the course of a term a choice between twelve short bursts, eight medium-length pieces or four longer assignments. The outcomes might be very similar but students have an overview of the work to be done and the choice of how to manage their time.

Exercise

Try this exercise with your students to get them used to using de Bono's thinking hats (de Bono, 1985).

Propositions

Discuss the proposition using de Bono's different ways of thinking. Try individual or group discussion, timed group brainstorms, listing ideas under each type of thinking, or asking students to create their own propositions for other groups to prepare for a debate between two sides.

Primary
Recycling is a waste of time and money. We should all just put our rubbish into a black bag and into a hole in the ground.

Secondary
Advertising aimed at children should be banned. Children are not mature enough to understand the tricks that advertisers use.

Further education
Heath and safety legislation gets in the way of good business. The Health and Safety Executive should be scrapped, individuals ought to be responsible for their own safety.

Hat	To ponder	Hat's response
Red	What are the feelings about this idea? What do I feel at this moment? What are my emotions, hunches, intuitions about this idea?	
Yellow	What are the benefits, values and advantages in this idea? What are the logical, positive points? What are the good things about the suggestions?	
Black	What are the points of caution? What are the disadvantages? What are the potential problems? What can go wrong? What are the logical, negative points? What are the difficulties surrounding the question?	

→

Hat	To ponder	Hat's response
Green	How can the idea be modified to improve it and to remove obvious faults? How can we overcome some of the difficulties that the black hat will point out? Are there alternative ways of achieving the same objective? What creative ideas do we have in this area?	
White	What facts and figures are useful for this idea? What information do I need? What information do we have?	
Blue	How have we been thinking about our thinking? Where are we now? Where are we going next? What kind of thinking should we do next?	

Exercise

Over the next few weeks of teaching see how much autonomy you can give to your students. Use the following table to record your progress.

This week my students will ...	Day	Group
Negotiate the configuration/layout of the desks and chairs		
Organise the room, rearrange the furniture		
Provide some of the resources for the lesson		
Distribute the resources		
Generate their own questions as well as their own answers		
Communicate their level of understanding to me using an agreed mechanism		
Have fewer questions but more time to think of the answers		
Engage in structured self-reflection		
Organise the make up and timing of their own groups		
Record reflective thoughts in diaries/blogs/books		

→

This week my students will...	Day	Group
Negotiate deadlines for homework and consequences for handing in on time and not handing in on time		
Lead small group/class discussion		
Be asked what they know about a subject before it is taught		
Put up a display of ideas		
Be scheduled in to contribute to or maintain a display		
Negotiate expectations for a task		
Negotiate success criteria for a task		
Create or contribute to their own 'learning map'		
Contribute to teaching a small group or the class		
Make choices about the time needed for activities		
Tidy up the room		
Give constructive feedback about the teaching		
Tell me what they have learned		

Critical questions

- How much responsibility for learning are your students allowed?

- Which elements of time planning can you negotiate with your students?

- What is your dominant role as a teacher: director? facilitator? mentor? coach? bystander?

Conclusion

By restricting personal autonomy we leave students with little responsibility for their learning. We take the responsibility away from them and leave ourselves with more work to do. A higher expectation of students to organise and develop their own learning leads to classrooms where the teacher has an oversight of assessment rather than absolute control over it. There are many different roles that a teacher may have without being judge, jury and sole assessor of achievement.

Key ideas summary

- Promoting and embedding autonomous learning can lead to a sea change in the quality of assessment in the classroom.

- In the workplace autonomy is central to our motivation. The same is true with students.

- Personalised learning is unattainable while the teacher is in control of the learning.

- Why do I take control over time when my students are better at it than me?

- Both teachers and students can learn strategies to manage time more effectively.

- Before everyone else finds out about how your students feel about your teaching, you might want to hear the feedback.

- Balanced self-reflection is at the heart of good mental health for teachers and students.

- Coloured hats and thinking from different angles helps students take control of their learning.

Going further

Go to the websites below to learn more about the ideas discussed in this chapter.

Edward de Bono: www.edwdebono.com/

Stephen Covey: www.stephencovey.com

Howard Gardner: www.howardgardner.com/

Naikan Self Reflection: www.todoinstitute.org/naikan.html

How far have we come?

The assessment tree

As autonomy is encouraged and the skills of independent assessment develop the tree gains structure and new growth is strong. Students branch out on their own developing new thoughts and directions.

Chapter

3

Teaching metacognition or 'knowing that you know!'

What this chapter will explore:

- Small changes to your practice that encourage and embed metacognitive thinking and processes

- Practical ways to use and share criteria to measure success

- Activities that allow students of all ages to engage in deeper thinking about how they learn

'The map was a record of our wanderings, and each time we returned we added to it or corrected it. It was, though a crude one, a representation of the area; we valued it as a cumulative record of our activities there. Furthermore, looking forward instead of back, the map set forth our expectations concerning this area we approached it a-fresh each time. By means of it we might hope to move around more purposefully, more intelligently.'

(James Britton, 1970)

Metacognition is not just a groovy word, it is at the heart of all learning theory. From Howard Gardner to Edward de Bono, from Vygotsky to Britton, from NLP to Accelerated Learning, the central theme is the same. Gaining a better understanding of how we think and learn helps us to direct thinking and questioning with more precision and purpose. It helps us to know what we know and in turn know what we don't know.

Good assessment relies on metacognitive skills from teachers as well as students. Metacognition refers to higher-order thinking which involves active control over the cognitive processes engaged in learning. Activities such as planning how to approach a given learning task, negotiating success criteria, monitoring comprehension and evaluating progress toward the completion of a task are metacognitive in nature.

Truly metacognitive classrooms are environments in which students will be able to tell you the level, grade or competency stage that they are on without prompting. They hold this information close not to impress visitors but because they are practised at understanding how they are progressing.

Measuring madness

Metcacognitve questioning is often introduced right at the end of a lesson and often narrowed to one question, 'What have we learned?' The required response to this question includes stock answers intended to satisfy the teacher by students who are keen to get out of the room and move on with their day. The truth is that *learning does not begin and end in 30-minute or one-hour time slots*.

Much to the frustration of the inspectorate, learning does not fit their tick-box criteria. As teachers we can fake it. We can design inspection lessons to show that everyone has reached their 'a-ha' or 'eureka!' or 'blimey!' moment at the same time. We can pretend that 30 minutes has been enough for learning to take place but we know that we are simply playing a game for other people to watch. When the observers and their clipboards are sent elsewhere we breathe a sigh of relief and go back to genuinely

→

---

differentiating learning. Sometimes in a single lesson I am satisfied if I have got the students engaged in the topic or theme, or thinking more globally about an issue, or elicited their emotion about a debate. I want my students to carry ideas between lessons but I am not going to lie to them and pretend that every lesson is a neat, compact 'learning experience' (don't get me started about such phrases).

The inspectorate demands that 'progress [their definition of learning] is demonstrable' in 20 minutes, but this lies in conflict with what we know about learning. Learning is more than good recall in the plenary. It is not proven by using the right key word at the right time or parroting the objectives back. It is not linear, predictable or even fully understood. It is wrong to encourage the notion that we can have control over when and how children learn. The honesty is taken out of what is happening. Teaching is reduced to absolutes: 'This is what you will learn in the next 30 minutes'. What we actually mean is, 'This is what I am going to try and embed in your working memory in the next 30 minutes'. The long-term memory needs more than just a single plenary. If we want to embed information and understanding in the long-term memory then students need to return to the information 90 minutes after the lesson, then tomorrow and perhaps again in two weeks. They must be allowed to embellish it, discuss it, re-examine what they remember. For the working memory you repeat to remember, for the long-term it is important that we remember to repeat.

The insistence on throwing everything into the working (short-term) memory does nothing for long-term learning. Instead of one plenary at the end of each lesson, lessons should be interleaved so that teachers run plenaries for each other.

Pretending that we have control over learning is leading us further down the dark data-driven, utterly accountable, unified methods path. Beware the 'units of learning' trolls who guard the bridge. They will try and convince you that all learning is quantifiable. They will take your soul and replace it with 'competences' without flinching.

Metacognitive habits and rituals

'Children must not only learn what to study, they must also learn how to study, and thus become confident, self-disciplined individuals capable of engaging in a lifelong process of learning knowledge, skills and understanding, which are the building blocks for secondary education and later life ... mental capital can be improved by using metacognitive strategies ... Metacognitive skills can be taught to very young children.'

(Rose, 2009)

Let's start a revolution by making some small, effortless changes that embed metacognitive habits in your daily teaching and drip feed responsibility for learning onto your students. Before you start introducing what you would like to teach, ask your students to spend a couple of minutes considering/noting/brainstorming/mapping ideas in response to at least one of the following questions:

- What do I know about this subject, topic, issue?

- Do I know what I need to know?

- Do I know where I can go to get some information/knowledge?

- How much time will I need to learn this?

- What are some strategies and tactics that I can use to learn this?

Try a simple column chart:

What we know	What we need to know	What we can find out

Find out what your students know before you teach them what you think they should know.

During the activity allow the students time for some metacognitive reflection by asking themselves:

- How will I know if I am learning at an appropriate rate?

- How can I spot an error if I make one?

- How should I revise my plan if it is not working to my expectations/satisfaction?

- Did I understand what I just heard, read or saw?

Competences

Encouraging students to gauge their own ability

Students can track and assess their own progress using a simple five-point scale adapted from the martial arts concept of the stages of leaning to mastery (Kirkpatrick and Kirkpatrick, 2006). Competency is rarely achieved quickly and certainly not within a 30-minute lesson. Consider learning a new skill:

1. Unconscious incompetence

The learner is unaware that he can not do a task.

For example, after watching an experienced juggler throwing and catching three balls a student exclaims 'I could do that', displaying little understanding of the skill level/knowledge/personal attributes and behaviour involved.

2. Conscious incompetence

The learner is aware of the task, but can not do it.

As the student learns to juggle he or she understands the pattern but can not replicate it.

3. Conscious competence

The learner is able to think through a task step-by-step and do it.

With practice the student recognises the faults in the pattern and how to adjust body position, throw and timing.

4. Unconscious competence

The learner can do the task without thinking about intermediate steps.

After more practice the student can juggle three balls continuously, then while holding a conversation, standing on one leg, etc.

5. Conscious unconscious competence

The highest level of competence is the *ability to do something without thinking about it, yet retain a level of awareness of how you do it*. This level of competence enables you to teach the skill to someone else.

In the example, the student is able to deconstruct what has been learned so that he or she can coach someone else and support their learning.

Why not try this?

Describe your current level of competence.

Rate and describe the level of competence demonstrated by your partner/group/ class.

Describe (next to steps 2–5) what you did/plan to do to move to this level.

5. Conscious unconscious competence

....

....

4. Unconscious competence

....

....

3. Conscious competence

....

....

2. Conscious incompetence

....

....

1. Unconscious incompetence

Figure 3.1

Introduce the students to the scale as steps on a ladder or as a practical example of your own learning. For older students you might like to map competences with the components of competency: skills, knowledge, behaviour and personal attributes. In a simple form you are beginning to establish a framework for assessment that the students can relate easily to. With younger children colour code the level of competency. Ask the students to place themselves on the scale at the start, during and at the final stages of a task. This is a more developed structure and sustained framework than 'what I have learned' at the end of the lesson. Regular checkpoints of 'How much have I learned and progressed' easily lead to 'What do I need to know/do next?'.

> **Why not try this?**
>
> Often it is the small things that make the difference. Try making a small change to the beginning of lessons that engages the students in thinking about what they know before they tackle the activity. Ask the students to rate themselves on a scale of 1–5:
>
> 1. I don't know anything about this.
>
> 2. I can do this task when there is somebody to help/guide/lead me.
>
> 3. I can do this task on my own.
>
> 4. I can help/guide/lead other people in this task.
>
> 5. I am a leading expert in this task.
>
> You might also ask students to anticipate the answer of their partner or even guess how they have rated each other. Use the numbers and descriptors as a reference point throughout the lesson: 'What steps do you think you need to take to move to 3?' 'Can you help Sandra, she thinks she is a 1 but I think she may be a 2 and just needs a little help.'

Metacognitive mobile mapping

Schools and colleges all over the world are banning students from using or bringing mobile phones into classrooms, as they are concerned about their misuse. They are worried about calls being made and received during lessons, about teachers being recorded in their worst moments, about cyber bullying, drug dealing, etc. Yet most modern phones have hardware built in and freely available software that is invaluable for students to record their own learning, their 'eureka moments', their questions, successes and challenges. The truth is that most students are already carrying around technology in their pocket that could be central to their learning if used appropriately. The problem is that many believe allowing phones to be used unrestricted in classrooms carries more risks than benefits.

The problems with mobile phones are with the behaviour of the user and not with the technology. We can teach students to use them appropriately. Just as a generation before we were told not to type 'Boobless' (55378008 upside down) on pocket calculators (I hope it was not just me), so today we can draw the appropriate boundaries for the use of mobile technology in classrooms. Within a few years, handsets could be replaced with discreet screens woven into clothing, earpieces without wires that are undetectable, and microphones that are so small that they are hidden from the teacher. When we can not see the technology it will be impossible to detect it let alone ban it. Mobile phones and cameras have already been designed into watches. Perhaps it is time to embrace the technology before students become so covert in their use of it that we can not police it.

A new generation of phones is being produced with projectors built in so that students can lead their own plenary for the group with photographs, audio clips and video mixed effortlessly into a presentation. The 3G network is growing and fast internet access via mobile phones is already with us.

Dip your toe in the water

Negotiate appropriate boundaries for the use of phones and try some or all of the following ideas:

- Students take five photographs and create a captioned collage of ideas from the task.

- Students record thoughts on their phones during a task and then use these ideas to evaluate their own progress.

- In pairs students video responses to plenary questions posed by their partner.

- Create a text message/'Twitter' summary of the lesson using fewer than, say 250, 150 or 50 characters

TOP TIP!

A word of warning – not all students have mobile phones. Some students will not bring their phones into class and some will not want to get theirs out. Some students live in a world where the mobile phone is as much about status as it is about calling people. Before embracing the phone as a tool for mapping learning make sure that no one is going to be shamed, embarrassed or excluded from the task.

Understanding examination/level criteria

Distributing published criteria to students with little or no explanation is not particularly helpful. It is not designed to be read by students and is not written in language that is necessarily accessible. Most students discard it, some are frightened by it, many don't understand it, and only a few find it mildly useful. The alternative is to spend hours rewriting the criteria in a 'student friendly' version. What emerges is often more confusing than the original document. Sometimes in the editing process decisions are made that can blunt the focus of the criteria, leaving it dumbed down and littered with low expectations. What is left after all the translation is often just as difficult to translate into the next step for learning.

The most valuable criteria is created by the students, guided by the teacher, built in stages and illustrated through display. It starts with simple questions, such as 'What do you think will make this successful?'

Why not try this?

Limit the criteria that you are working with at any one time.

Create more focus by dissecting a single criterion into skills, knowledge and understanding headings and using these to assess against.

Simple key words/lists. As the lesson progresses reinforce the students who are meeting the agreed criteria with ticks, stickers or students' names alongside.

Learning styles questionnaires

Learning styles questionnaires provide a useful starting point for thinking about how we learn. Most students have completed such questionnaires at one time or another and it is not uncommon to be introduced to a student who will tell you that they are one type of learner or another. The well-intentioned questionnaire has been translated as absolute science and a 'fait accompli'. We all have the capacity to learn and adapt to new ways of learning. Some aspects of how we prefer to learn may be constant and others different on a Monday morning to how they are on a Wednesday afternoon. Some students with certain preferences today may well develop others in years to come. The questionnaires are therefore a starting point but certainly not an end in themselves.

Thinking about the brain

Learning about how the brain functions is appropriate for even very young children. There are scientific approaches and highly creative approaches that can work separately or alongside each other. Sometimes a firm foundation of scientific knowledge can give more meaning to the creative approaches.

The attraction of the mind map or brainstorm or, more recently, mind shower is that it starts to create order out of the chaos of the creative flow. Mind mapping is a well-used technique. Here it is translated to deeper metacognitive thought about how the brain thinks and learns. I have used this exercise with students of all ages and abilities, and with parents and teachers.

Sculpting the brain

Use Play-doh, Plasticine or coloured clay to create simple models of the brain. Split the different parts and functions of the brain into different colours. Create three-dimensional sculptures of the brain using Figure 3.2 as a starting point.

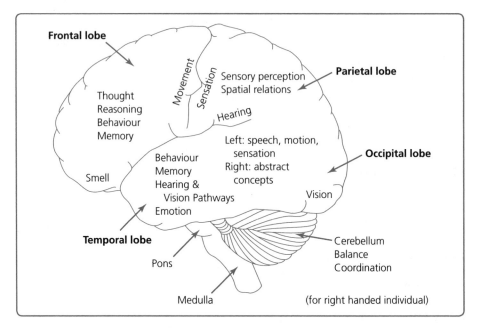

Figure 3.2: Lobes of the brain

Ask students to remodel the sculpture in relation to their own brain, a partner's, a family member's, a famous musician's, etc.

These models can be displayed and referred to throughout the lesson. The elasticity of the brain is emphasised and how the brain grows over the course of the year/module can be imagined and visualised.

Creatively mapping the brain

Asking students to reflect on how they think their own brain thinks and how thinking is linked together opens up some great opportunities for discussions around learning and thinking. Asking students to do the same exercise for another person is revealing. Inviting them to create a diagram of your brain is a gentle risk worth taking.

Using a basic two-dimensional outline of the shape of the brain (see Figure 3.3) you might start with: 'What types of thinking go on in the brain?' Or for younger students you could ask 'What is in your brain?' and allow them to use whatever words, colours or images they think fit. Collect ideas as a class or small group. Consider the sizes of a the different areas. Is there more creativity than logic in your brain? Less emotion, more rational thought? More speaking or more listening? Now how will you create groupings, which areas interrelate/which are linked/which are interdependent. How do these groups represent your interests, your relationships, your character?

Students should compare the maps with a partner. Swap maps and make changes to each other's. Display the maps with tracing paper overlays so that you can add and change them as the term/course/module progresses. Refer to the brains during discussions to encourage students to reflect on their thinking skills and to take responsibility for refining skills in certain types of thinking. Create the brain hats as explained below to extend the image into 3D.

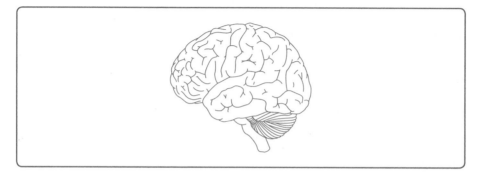

Figure 3.3

Changing your brain!

'We can take advantage of our brain's plasticity and train it.'

(Richard Davidson, professor of psychiatry and psychology at University of Wisconsion, Madison)

Davidson and colleagues were the first researchers to use functional magnetic resonance imaging (fMRI) to indicate that positive emotions such as loving–kindness and compassion can be learned in the same way as playing a musical instrument or being proficient in a sport (Lutz *et al.*, 2008). Scans revealed that brain circuits used to detect emotions and feelings were dramatically changed in subjects who had extensive experience practising compassional meditation. Learning to juggle alters the structure of motion detection areas in the brain within as little as seven days. It seems practice might make more than just perfect. Even in the context of skills that are repetitive this is fascinating. Consider students learning the Qur'ān and their ability to learn by rote. How much have they developed the areas of the brain connected with language, memory or rhythm?

The idea that the brain is elastic is important in terms of the expectations of students and staff, social mobility and perceived ceilings of achievement.

Study skills

The idea of study skills comes to many students in the first term of their final year of GCSEs when a company comes in to lead Year 11 in a 'Study Skills' workshop. These workshops are great for motivating students to study and revise. They give a strong focus to revision skills and managing time and effort as students prepare for exams. Yet in some schools this is the only focus on study skills. Rather than being a useful reminder and refresher the workshops are often the first time that students are taught the skills that they need for self study. Of course it is too late for many students and it is far more productive to integrate these skills from the beginning of schooling rather that waiting for an exam and rush to patch the skills gap.

Deliberately teach and nuture study habits with your students daily.

> **TOP TIP!**
>
> Try giving your students a task to complete at home and ask them to record exactly how they accomplished it. Students should record the process that they went through – where they did the task, whose help they asked for, how many sittings they took to do it, what they ate, drank or listened to while they did it, what time of day it was done, what distractions they had. As part of the deconstruction of the process students can discuss their working process, compare different ways of working with different grades awarded for the work, and adopt the working processes of other students to try out.

How can students gain self-efficacy?

Self-efficacy is commonly defined as the belief in one's capabilities to achieve a goal or an outcome. Students with a strong sense of efficacy are more likely to challenge themselves with difficult tasks and be intrinsically motivated. There are four sources of self-efficacy. Teachers can use strategies to build self-efficacy in various ways, as shown in the following list based on Margolis and McCabe (2004) and Bandura (1994):

1. **Mastery experiences:** Students' successful experiences boost self-efficacy, while failures erode it. This is the most robust source of self-efficacy.

2. **Vicarious experience:** Observing a peer succeed at a task can strengthen beliefs in one's own abilities.

3. **Verbal persuasion:** Teachers can boost self-efficacy with credible communication and feedback to guide the student through the task or motivate them to make their best effort.

4. **Emotional state**: A positive mood can boost one's beliefs in self-efficacy, while anxiety can undermine it. A certain level of emotional stimulation can create an energising feeling that can contribute to strong performances. Teachers can help by reducing stressful situations and lowering anxiety surrounding events like exams or presentations.

Examples of teacher strategies

- Insist that students monitor their own learning and thinking. Provide simple mechanisms for them to achieve this.

- Teach and highlight study strategies as part of class, home and coursework.

- Guide students in relating ideas to existing knowledge structures.

- Have students develop questions, asking questions of themselves and about what's going on around them ('Have you asked a good question today?').

- Help students to know when to ask for help. (They must be able to self-monitor – require students to show how they have attempted to deal with the problem of their own).

- Show students how to transfer knowledge, attitudes, values, skills to other situations or tasks.

Think aloud protocol

The think aloud protocol developed by Clayton Lewis (Lewis and Rieman, 1994) involves participants thinking aloud as they are performing a set of specified tasks. Users are asked to say whatever they are looking at, thinking, doing and feeling as they go about their task. This enables observers to see first hand the process of task completion (rather than only its final product).

Observers at such a test are asked to objectively take notes of everything that users say, without attempting to interpret their actions and words. Test sessions are often audio and video taped so that developers can go back and refer to what participants did, and how they reacted. The purpose of this method is to make explicit what is implicitly present in subjects who are able to perform a specific task.

Used as part of formative assessment the think aloud protocol reveals the approach to learning as well as the success with it.

Strategy spotlight

Get down with da kidz

Something happens to the dynamic in the room when you place a large sheet of paper on the floor with students sitting around. Something that can not be replicated by collating ideas on the screen. Once you are established as a cartographer for the group the responsibility for thinking settles with the students. You map ideas, choices and pathways for the students. Help them to design a map, a coding, an order for their thinking, mix and filter ideas, words and thoughts. Physically something has changed. You have given them a sense of control and power, yet demonstrated your confidence and trust. They are looking down on you yet you have become one of the group, learning with them and through them.

Reflecting on practice

The Thinkenstein project

Promoting metacognitive thinking and understanding of how individuals learn is simpler with older students of higher ability. They are able to understand the concepts, skills and language and run with new frameworks with little support. For younger children, and particularly those with learning

→

difficulties, things are not so straightforward. In a three-year project with mainstream and special schools in Birmingham on practical approaches to metacognition, we were charged with researching and developing this meta-cognitive teaching with LSAs, teachers, head teachers and children in Year 4.

We developed the idea of using a proxy self that could be used by the individual yet was common to the whole class. The monster 'Thinkenstein' was born. Once established, the proxy allowed students to engage in metacognitive activities while choosing whether to relate to themselves. Thinkenstein needed to be created, to think and be taught to think. He needed brain chips to be designed, and then linked and combined for thinking. Sensory worlds to interact with were created, huge colour-coded maps of thinking produced, language filtered and programmed. We experimented with different frameworks, such as Belle Wallace's TASC model, Pivotal's Negotiated Assessment Grids (see Chapter 6), Gardner's Multiple Intelligences and de Bono's Thinking Skills, while persistently pursuing metacognitive thinking.

Figure 3.4: TASC model

Source: Copyright © Belle Wallace 2000. Reproduced with permission

In summer schools run with LSAs over three years, daily metacognitive rituals were established and negotiated: regular checkpoints for self-reflection, daily physical warm-ups, lots of decision making and autonomy for the students, peer assessment and teaching, maps of learning that flooded (and

→

at times overwhelmed) the classroom, and enough adults to support the full range of ability. We had the luxury of freedom from curriculum and a high teacher:student ratio that you don't have in the classroom. Yet the children did not find it difficult to adapt to new ways of working. They were fascinated by the idea of what was in their heads (or Thinkenstein's), by the idea of a monster that was learning and was theirs to design and control.

Metacognitive thinking and questioning came easily, naturally. Those students with limited spoken language found and were helped to find ways of representing ideas, those with hearing and sight impairment touched and heard their way through. They created fascinating worlds to teach the monster new ideas and ways of thinking. They became scientists analysing experiments and testing hypotheses. Thinkenstein was always gentle and funny, not a modern Frankenstein's monster, more of a very friendly robot/human/Lego man. Maps of his brain and the children's brains were drawn and compared. Parents and grandparents were asked to create a map of their own brain, which promoted strong engagement and discussion.

Thinkenstein lives and still lives in many classrooms. A safe proxy to introduce metacognition, as simple or as complex as you want to make him.

Practical strategies for primary, secondary and further education

Primary

Brain hats

Each student will need a strip of paper as a band that goes around the head. Light cardboard works better to give a firmer structure. Cut the first strip 60 cm long and 4 cm wide, turn it into a band that fits around the head and trim to fit.

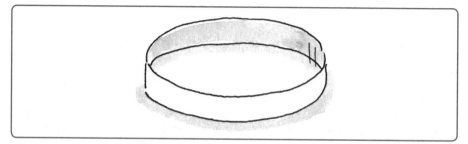

Figure 3.5

Attach two strips that cross in the middle using glue or sticky tape onto this circular band.

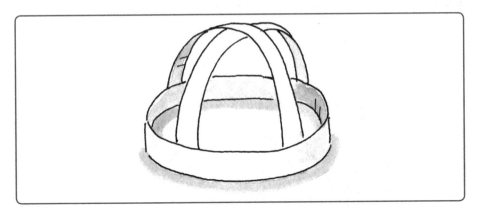

Figure 3.6

Now attach eight equally spaced strips to the inside of the band so that they hang down like dreadlocks from the hat.

Figure 3.7

Now take the unattached ends and attach to the centre top of the hat. They should be long enough to create a tight curl. If they are too saggy the hat will wobble uncontrollably, which is funny, but does not make a useable hat.

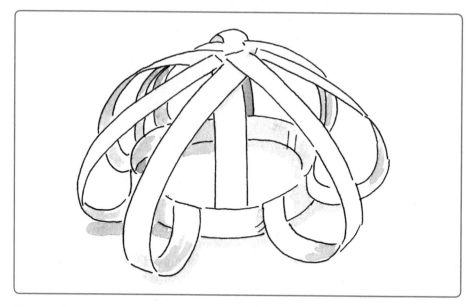

Figure 3.8

Finally create your brain:

- Use coloured tissue paper to demarcate different areas of the brain.

- Use paper to fill in the gaps in the hats with sub-sections.

- Think about the proportions of the brain – how big is your sports thinking compared to number thinking?

- Connect areas of the brain with coloured wool.

- Hang symbols from different areas to indicate special skills.

Secondary

Metacognitive spinners

These are simple spinners made from an octagonal piece of card with a pencil through the middle. Label with different types of thinking, questions, prompts, sentence starters or success criteria. Now use discussion, peer assessment, self reflection.

Thinking posts

Children should write different thoughts on different coloured sticky notes, for example something I understand on red, something that I don't on yellow and a question I have on green. They can then post them in designated places in the room.

Multiple intelligences

Use multiple intelligences to frame different types of thinking and learning. As a plenary, use the different intelligences written on differently coloured paper to allow you to reflect on the intelligences used and how they overlap. Students should write down the different intelligences that they used and how they used them, and place the ideas on the relevant pieces of paper.

Further education/post-16

Deeper thinking

With older students, the following categories might help them enjoy the deeper learning after the initial 'hook' of the creative brain mapping or making task:

abstract thinking	instinct	picture thinking
analogy	intelligence	prediction
attitude	introspection	premise
calculation	knowledge management	problem finding
categorisation	language	problem shaping
cognition	lateral thinking	problem solving
cognitive restructuring	linguistics	proposition
common sense	logic	rationality
concept	logical argument	reason
conjecture	logical assertion	reasoning
concrete concepts	meaning (linguistics)	reasoning event
critical thinking	meaning (non-linguistic)	self-reflection
deductive reasoning	meaning (semiotics)	sapience
definition	mental calculation	stream of consciousness
estimation	mental function	systems intelligence
evaluation	metacognition	systems thinking
explanation	mind's eye	thinking maps
historical thinking	mindset	thinking process
hypothesis	multiple intelligences	thought experiment
idea	multitasking	visual thinking
identification (information)	pattern matching	working memory
inference	personality	writing

Exercise

Fill in the percentages from this famous William Glasser quotation –10%, 20%, 30%, 50%, 70%. 80%, 95% – (answer at the end).

How we Learn

_____	of what we HEAR
_____	of what we TEACH TO SOMEONE ELSE
_____	of what we SEE and HEAR
_____	of what we READ
_____	of what is EXPERIENCED PERSONALLY
_____	of what we SEE
_____	of what is DISCUSSED with OTHERS

What does Glasser's scale suggest about the way that we structure learning for students?

What does it suggest about the way that we organise schools, colleges and individual classrooms?

How could you restructure your next lesson to fit Glasser's research?

Answer to the exercise

10% of what we READ, 20% of what we HEAR, 30% of what we SEE, 50% of what we SEE and HEAR, 70% of what is DISCUSSED with OTHERS, 80% of what is EXPERIENCED PERSONALLY, 95% of what we TEACH TO SOME-ONE ELSE.

(www.williamglasser.com)

Critical questions

- When can you invest time in metacognitive activities that encourage a deeper understanding about how individuals learn?
- How can you create a proxy for students who initially find it difficult to think about their own thinking?
- What visual reminders will you create with students to sustain metacognitive thinking?

Conclusion

Encouraging a heightened sense of how we think and learn makes learners more reflective. It gives students confidence to tackle new challenges and control their thoughts when they experience frustrations. Mapping criteria with students allows them to take control of where they are going and how they are going to learn their way there.

Key ideas summary

- Good assessment relies on metacognitive skills from teachers as well as students.

- Learning does not begin and end in 30-minute or one-hour time slots.

- Find out what your students know before you teach them what you think they should know.

- Teachers are cartographers for their students mapping ideas, choices and pathways.

- The problems with mobile phones are with the behaviour of the user and not with the technology.

- The most valuable criteria is created by the students, guided by the teacher, built in stages and illustrated through display.

Going further

Belle Wallace: www.nace.co.uk

Learning styles questionnaire: www.vark-learn.com

How far have we come?

The assessment tree

Metacognitive strategies give confidence and add skills to autonomous learners. The branches of the tree grow rapidly away from the trunk as students find they are increasingly responsible for their own learning.

Practical strategies for peer assessment

What this chapter will explore:

- Strategies to sharpen peer assessment making it productive and efficient
- How consistently clear boundaries and high expectations can set a high standard for private peer work
- How peer assessment is as important for the assessor as the assessed

'Knowledge speaks, but wisdom listens.'

(Jimi Hendrix)

Assessment is not just a set of processes or a final mark but a series of opportunities to encourage and build on successful learning. It is more about the conversation than the paperwork, more about the agreed target than the mark. Train your students to give clear structured assessment of their peers with productive conversations that build relationships. When executed rigorously, peer assessment helps both parties to understand the next step in their learning. Lazy peer assessment, without structure or sharp focus, is just another 5 minutes of conversation about the football or the weekend. Peer assessment is not an afterthought or bolt-on for the inspectors but an essential motor for a productive and efficient classroom. Meaningful peer assessment does not just summarise or discuss, but extends learning.

Being able to hold the mirror up for others, while maintaining a good relationship, is a critical skill for teachers and students. Yet there are a number of common problems associated with peer assessment. The main concern for teachers is that the process is not visible. While we can not control conversations or be 100 per cent certain that the process is as productive as it should be, we can create the conditions that make it difficult for students to drift off-task. We can set and negotiate boundaries, encourage certain behaviours and make time for peer assessment. We can make our peer assessment more productive and remove ourselves as the sole arbiter of success and failure. When students invest in their own learning they begin to own their own behaviour.

Within the process there are issues with the attitudes that students bring to peer assessment: students who know each other so well that they are off-task in a heartbeat, students who find it difficult to even acknowledge one another, students who have little experience of developing conversations about learning, students who find it difficult to voice their opinions, students who are too fragile to accept a critical eye and students who are too blunt in their assessment of the work of others. Successful and, moreover, useful peer assessment that actually raises achievement can not be left to chance. It has to be so much more than 'Discuss each other's work in pairs for a few minutes' (while I try to get the projector working). It must be structured, taught with reference to skills and strategies, accountable, and supported with simple frameworks for conversation and feedback.

We all remember the difficulties of childhood and teenage relationships. In any class there are students who would rather not work with each other and some who actively seek anonymity. Take control of the decisions on pairings as you take control of your seating plan. Make it clear that your expectation is that everyone will assess for and with each other and refuse to pander to the prejudices, friendships and preconceptions of your students. To begin with you need to take the responsibility away from them: some will protest but most of your students will feel more secure knowing that they can blame the groupings on you: 'I know, I didn't want to work with her either, *he* made me.'

Setting a strong model

Before asking your students to pair up and launch into sensitive conversations about their learning, spend time demonstrating and deconstructing a model of what you want. Try using the following ideas:

- The teacher playing the role of the student, providing a realistic model.

- An audio recording of an assessment conversation between peers.

- A live performance using two students. Ask the audience to reflect what is working and to step in and show how it might be improved.

- A video recording of students from last year/parallel classes.

It is vital that that you include strong examples of the standard that you expect. Ask your students to deconstruct the model, agree a list of success criteria and negotiate standards of conduct. Refer to this standard before you ask the students to embark on peer assessment. Display it as text, icons or photographs of students with captions, or on the screen as a slide. Reinforce the agreed expectation persistently.

TOP TIP!

Spend time agreeing the boundaries and expectations. Ask them the question 'What makes a good think, pair, share?' for younger children (students think individually for 30 seconds/1 minute then pair up to share and compare their thoughts, see Practical strategies, p. 71) or 'What makes a peer assessment useful?' A good place to start is 'Tell me how you like to receive feedback on your work'.

With your students, agree what works and in turn what to avoid. Use this information as a basis for your 'Guide to Peer Assessment' display or handout. Discuss with students the idea of 3:1 feedback (see Chapter 1), or the bad news sandwich ('sandwiching' the criticism between two positive reflections of the work). Try to agree a simple formula for feedback, a straightforward ritual that can be applied to all situations, as in the box below.

Why not try this?

Rituals and routines take some of the anxiety away from conversations about learning. Students like the predictable, safe and structured nature of the conversation that flows from a negotiated and agreed ritual. Keep the routine simple,

→

---

clear, prominently displayed and referred to throughout the lesson. Frame the routine positively by identifying the behaviours that you want to see. Give your energy to catching students who are following the routine and positively reinforce their behaviour. For example, in a primary classroom this might be:

1. Shake hands and say hello.

2. Look at each other while you are talking.

3. Talk about what went well first.

4. Then talk about what could be changed to make it better.

In secondary:

1. Search for what works, what is good, what has been achieved.

2. Be kind in your feedback, give bad news gently.

3. Feedback on the work not on the person.

And for older/more able students:

1. 3:1 positive comment to constructive criticism.

2. Justify at least three examples by comparing with the exemplar materials.

3. Agree three written targets for redrafting.

Do not rest until you have peer assessment that is rigorous, intelligent and respectful. Refuse to accept lazy conversations just as you refuse to accept incomplete homework. Few teachers give real emphasis to modelling, negotiating and setting high expectations for peer assessment. Fewer still take time to break down the expectations into specific behaviours that need to be observed. If you embed the expectation at this stage and establish it as a high priority, your students will have the right foundations to make peer assessment genuinely useful. After a couple of weeks the pressure for the teacher to assess everything will subside. Students will naturally begin to consult each other. By the end of term the sea of hands or queue at your desk will have significantly reduced. Great. Take some time out. Sit back and watch your students teaching each other.

Students marking each other's work

- Agree success criteria with the students, using their own language in the first instance.

- Agree clear guidance for the markers – how to mark, and acceptable/unacceptable comments.

- Try anonymous scripts to moderate the marking – research shows how the rank order of marking changes dramatically when teachers know which students submitted the work.

- Use work from past students to mark. The markers can then compare their grading with actual grades and discuss variations.

- Focus on one success criteria and break it down into the constituent parts for intensive assessment of a single aspect.

- Display a number of pieces of work with the students marking in teams. Each student looks for a certain aspect of the agreed criteria.

- Play speed marking with teams in competition to find where the marks have been earned or lost.

Presentations and performances

When students are asked to present their work to the class, the feedback is usually given to the group as a whole. Just as with 'desk' work some students quickly learn work-avoidance tactics and lean heavily on those who have a natural presence in front of an audience. Students who have contributed little to the presentation can remain hidden, avoiding the performance and the feedback. There are small changes to the routine that can ensure all students are involved, engaged and accountable for their contribution.

Before the first group presents their work, ask the students in the audience to identify one student who they will watch carefully throughout the presentation.

Usually what happens when a class of students presents in groups is that you respond enthusiastically to the first few but by the time you have sat through the eighth version of the same thing the will to live is seeping from you and you can barely muster an enthusiastic, 'Well that was … interesting'. Establish the ritual and make each student in the audience responsible for giving feedback to another student. Ask the students to pair up and clarify the criteria that are to be assessed, so that the whole experience becomes much more about learning than crowd control. Meaningful individual feedback emerges, with – you will be relived to know – less emphasis on your hastily improvised summary judgement.

The students in the audience will need to prepare in their heads or write down three aspects of the performance/presentation that met the agreed criteria, as well as suggesting an area for improvement. You might agree the criteria as a class before the presentations or students can pair up beforehand to spend a minute agreeing the individual criteria.

As each performance ends ask the audience to prepare what they are going to say and then go and have their conversation with their partner. Everyone works simultaneously so that no single voice can be heard in the room. Wander amongst the feedback and collect snippets of conversations that you can use to reinforce the agreed standard. Once students realise that they can not avoid scrutiny, their motivation towards the task will shift. It is easy to hide in a group presentation when the assessment is about the group, but not so easy when you know that you are being scrutinised individually.

This pedagogy is useful for relationship building. You can manipulate it so that students who have never before looked each other in the eye are required to interact respectfully, and even positively.

Strategy spotlight

Are you waiting to talk or are you listening?

Concentrating on the finer rituals or manners of formal conversation sets a high standard for the quality of listening as well as speaking. Define the skills, attitudes and manners of listening and use it as a checklist. We listen with our eyes, our body language, our 'umms' and 'mmms' and 'rights'. Good listeners are not waiting for their turn to speak or trying to think of a parallel example from their own lives. Good listeners are listening and questioning to understand, not to compare, to solve or to judge. They look attentive, sit forward, perhaps turn their head to the side. Good listeners are seeking to learn, not simply to 'return serve'.

Teaching active listening

'We listen with our bodies, our eyes, our 'errs' and 'ums.'

Reflected feelings

You show you have been listening and understand what they have been saying, e.g. 'So you are feeling … ', 'You felt that … '.

Backchannelling

Human speakers rely on the listener 'backchanelling', using 'ums', 'rights', 'uh huhs', 'mmms', nods, smiles and 'yups'. The responses help the speaker to know that he or she is being understood, reinforce that the listener is interested and listening, and reflects agreement or disagreement.

Paraphrasing

This is a way of restating what has been said but in a different way. It allows you to check that you have heard correctly, shows that you are still listening, and encourages further exploration of the problem, e.g. 'As I understand it ... ', 'You seem to be saying ... '.

Focusing

This allows you to focus on particular issues/problems by asking specific questions to get specific information, e.g. 'Tell me about ... ', 'What do you feel when ... '.

The use of all these skills begins to establish a relationship and allows you to explore the problem from the other person's point of view.

Peer feedback genres

Spice up peer assessment for students who are well practised at it by giving them genres to play with. Why not try the following:

Listen ...

'As carefully as someone who is just learning the language'

'As if you are hanging on every word'

'As if true wisdom has been revealed to you'

'As if all of the information is of vital (secret mission) importance

Write ...

'A postcard home'

'A note to an important client'

'A set of bullet points in an email'

'A report from an examiner'

'A review of the work in a newspaper'

'A blog entry'

Reflecting on practice

A school right in the middle of a Bangladeshi and Pakistani community is a fascinating place to work. The divide between the boys and the girls was only ever crossed in the classroom and then with some fear and trepidation. The clash between conservative Muslim values and modern teaching was highlighted in more active subjects. The boys didn't want to work with the girls. The girls, to their credit, were generally not particularly bothered who they worked with, but the boys did not want to be seen talking to, let alone performing a scene with them. Teaching behind desks was generally less problematic than teaching actively, in open spaces and with exercises that demanded physical contact. At first it would be like a scene from a teenage disco with the boys on one side and the girls on the other. I had come from a school where there was no such divide. In fact we spent a great deal of time trying to get the older male and female students to keep their hands off each other. It became quickly apparent that I was teaching two classes in one.

I set about trying to make some changes but faced resistance from the beginning. I realised that I needed to bridge the chasm between the genders with some deeper understanding of the cultural divide and by introducing some low-risk active tasks in a very structured environment.

The first task was to find a basis in Islam for the argument that we should learn together. This was remarkably easy. Although not from the Holy Qur'ān the following quotation is widely attributed to the Holy Prophet (PBUH). I quoted it often:

'Acquire knowledge even if you have to travel to China'.

Another, perhaps more authentic comment on the value of education is found in the Holy Qur'ān:

'The Prophet said, 'He who has a slave-girl and teaches her good manners and improves her education and then manumits and marries her, will get a double reward; and any slave who observes Allah's right and his master's right will get a double reward'.
(Translation of *Sahih Bukhari*, Manumission of Slaves, Volume 3, Book 46, Number 723)

The value of education for all is clear. Go as far as you need to go and do whatever is necessary to educate yourself. Including, in my classroom, working alongside others regardless of their gender. I tested the rationale with a few key parents and they cautiously agreed. To show them what kinds of activities I had in mind, I invited a few to watch a lesson with a group of younger students, who were less conscious of the gender divide than the older groups. The parents gave me some advice, taught me the boundaries for appropriate physical contact, and this gave me a strong basis for making changes with the students.

→

Alongside the construction of a strong argument I began planning activities that encouraged conversations about learning, practical paired work, mixed-gender performances and, eventually, safe physical contact between male and female students. The inevitable protestations of the boys were gently subdued. After all, I had the support of voices far more powerful than my own. Over the course of two years we all 'travelled to China' many times with remarkable work emerging and the usually boisterous boys portraying sensitive and even subordinate characters with confidence.

I learned a great deal about Islam, faith, community and Muslim culture during that time, often by revealing my ignorance and being corrected by patient students. Introducing an English GCSE module on the death penalty I led with the big question 'Who has the right over life and death, the state or the individual?' This was the question that the entire project was to investigate. Asif patiently raised his hand, 'Allah has the right over life and death' and there was a unanimous nod of agreement. The 12-week scheme of work was done in under 12 seconds.

Practical strategies for primary, secondary and further education

Primary

Think, pair, share

A well-established beginners' ritual that encourages students to take a moment to consider what they are going to say and how they are going to respond, before they pair up and share thoughts about the work or task.

Assessing with symbols and scores

Hand-held Olympic-style scorecards are fun but as with any scoring mechanism the marks must have meaning. Agree a scale with the students before the group begins marking and relate this to the specific criteria that are being assessed.

Secondary

Complex scoring

More complex scoring systems might mirror those in gymnastics, where technical difficulty, style, presentation can be assessed. Modern judging and scoring formats come from television shows such as *Strictly Come Dancing*. The table overleaf gives an example of a scorecard you could use.

Scorecard for a presentation	Totals
Vocal control	1 2 3 4 5 6 7 8 9 10
Visual aids	1 2 3 4 5 6 7 8 9 10
Presentation style	1 2 3 4 5 6 7 8 9 10
Engaging the audience	1 2 3 4 5 6 7 8 9 10
Involving the audience	1 2 3 4 5 6 7 8 9 10
Technical difficulty	1 2 3 4 5 6 7 8 9 10
Passion for the topic	1 2 3 4 5 6 7 8 9 10
Evidence of research	1 2 3 4 5 6 7 8 9 10
Confidence with the material	1 2 3 4 5 6 7 8 9 10
Knowledge of the subject	1 2 3 4 5 6 7 8 9 10
Justification for the overall score	

Anonymous peer assessment

A gallery of excerpts from written work to assess and link to the criteria with pins and string – use student-created criteria and then link them with grade/level descriptors.

Developing and extending peer conversations with fortune tellers

Even adults enjoy the movement of the fortune teller. Sometimes the smallest and most frivolous things spark motivation and concentration.

Many students will meet the expectations for structuring discussions and giving focused feedback but will need support in developing the conversation. Support students to get the most out of peer assessment by using the fortune tellers as part of peer questioning.

Introduce students to the 'Could you?' stems and ask them to select some for their fortune tellers. They can number the outside flaps, use images, colours, key words, etc. The questions are written inside the fortune teller:

Could you … ?

List, define, tell, describe, identify, show, name, summarise, describe, interpret, contrast, predict, estimate, differentiate, discuss, extend, illustrate, show, examine, relate, separate, order, explain, arrange, divide, compare, integrate, rearrange, compose, formulate, generalise, decide, rank, grade, measure, recommend, convince, select, judge, discriminate, conclude.

(Adapted from Bloom, 1969)

Making a fortune teller

You will need a square piece of paper. A 15 cm × 15 cm square works well.

1. Fold the piece of paper in half across the diagonal. Undo this fold. Fold in half again across the other diagonal. Undo this fold too. The point at which these two folds meet marks the centre of the square.

2. Take one corner and fold it into the middle of the square. Repeat this for the three remaining corners.

3. Turn the paper over.

4. Again take one corner and fold it into the middle of the square. Repeat this for the three other corners.

5. Now, keeping the same side facing up, fold the paper in half, by folding the side of the square closest to you over to the side that is furthest away from you. Your paper should now be a rectangular shape.

6. Now undo this fold, rotate the paper through 90 degrees and repeat step 5 with the side that is now closest to you.

7. Keeping the paper folded into this rectangle, lift it off the table and put your thumbs and index fingers inside the flaps on the front and back of each side of the paper, gripping it.

8. Now squeeze the paper in so that all four finger tips meet. The fortune teller will then take shape.

9. You can now label the fortune teller and use it. On each of the four flaps, write the name of one colour (e.g. red, blue, green, yellow).

10. Turn over the flaps, so they are now face down. This will reveal four large triangles and eight smaller ones. On each of the eight smaller triangles, write a random number.

11. Open up the larger triangles, to display eight smaller triangles divided by a fold. On each of these triangles write a question (see the list above for ideas).

12. The fortune teller is now ready for use.

How to play

1. Hold the fortune teller with your thumbs and index fingers on the four flaps. Ask a friend to select one of the colours written on the four flaps. Spell out that colour while moving your thumbs and index fingers back and forth in alternating directions.

2. Ask your friend to select one of the numbers that they see. Count out that number while moving your thumbs and index fingers back and forth in alternating directions.

3. Ask your friend to choose another number that they see. Open the large triangle that corresponds to the number that they chose and read the question.

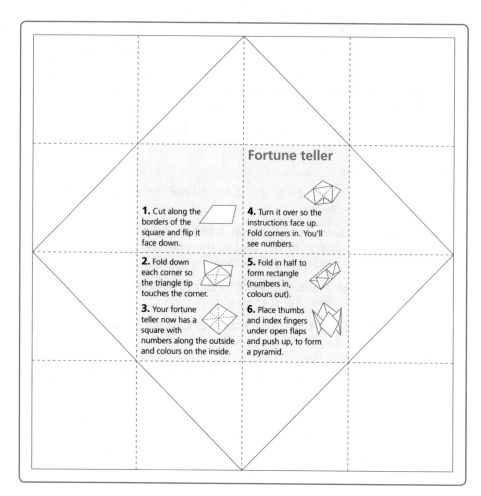

Figure 4.1

Further education/post-16

Old hands

Use students who have already taken their exams to provide exemplar materials for practical work. You might use your Year 13 to video themselves working through a Year 12 project in order to provide examples of the skills and attitudes for work in grade boundaries progress and final assessment. An A level group might create a map of 'What I wish I'd known when I started the course' .Year 13 might prepare a lesson, video guide or booklet for Year 12 on how to survive AS.

Exercise

Students who are not used to talking to each other let alone assessing for each other can build trust through safe, structured public interaction. Here are some simple exercises that get students talking, having fun, laughing, building trust and breaking preconceptions. 'Carousels' and 'four-line plays' are dead certs. Save time discussing, negotiating and managing trust issues by investing time in play.

For each exercise the same configuration is needed. An inner circle of students stand or sit facing an outer circle of students who are facing in. Everyone has a partner. The inner wheel does not move, but the outer wheel does. You can use this configuration in different ways.

Carousels

Ask a question that has many possible answers. Partners share an idea each then the outer wheel rotates one position clockwise. The new partners share an idea each and so on. The teacher or another student stands in the middle and collects ideas for a plenary or summary of the best ideas. This can also be used for discussing all views on a single issue. Each pair is given one minute on each question before the outer wheel moves round.

Four-line plays

Each student has two lines to speak, making a four-line conversation. The first line is spoken by the student in the inner circle (A) and then in turn by the student in the outer circle (B). Keep the lines short, open to interpretation and easy to remember. An example would be:

A   'What was that?'

B   'What?'

A   'That noise'

B   'Oh no'

Now play with the conversation. Try the following:

- Change the meaning by the way each line is said: whispering, screaming.
- Suggest different emotions: fear, excitement, religious fervour.
- Different speeds: slow and desperate/fast and furious.
- Different situations: through a keyhole, during a power cut, on a small boat.

→

- Ask the students to continue the exercise without speaking.
- Ask the students to greet each other in as many different ways as possible using words and touch: shake hands, high five, 'gangsta' style (series of hand gymnastics in an unfathomable sequence!).

Critical questions

- What will the pay-off be if your students are taught to peer assess effectively?
- How are you going to establish high expectations and prioritise peer assessment?
- How many of your students avoid working with each other? How would they benefit from working, at different times, with all students?

Conclusion

Pursue standards that you have agreed in peer assessment vigorously. Skilled peer assessors raise their own achievement and the achievement of those that they work with. Your workload is significantly reduced when your students take responsibility for assessing each other.

Key ideas summary

- Peer assessment is not an afterthought or bolt-on for inspectors but an essential motor for a productive and efficient classroom.
- Make it clear that your expectation is that everyone will assess for and with each other and refuse to pander to the prejudices, friendships and preconceptions of your students.
- Spend time demonstrating and deconstructing a model of what you want, and set your expectations high.
- Refuse to accept lazy conversations just as you refuse to accept incomplete homework.
- Establish a simple routine with the students.
- Support students to get the most out of peer assessment by drip-feeding ideas for questioning that extends.

How far have we come?

The assessment tree

Maturing branches show students working together to support each other's development.

Negotiated target setting

What this chapter will explore:

- Strategies for passing responsibility for target setting successfully to your students

- How to negotiate targets with students so that they are meaningful, owned and acted upon

- How to help students manage the number and scope of the targets they are striving for

'You teach a child to read and he or she will be able to pass a literacy test.'

(George W. Bush, 21 February 2001)

Writing targets for other people isn't productive. To motivate people to strive to achieve a target they need to be fully involved. Not in agreeing the target or accepting your advice but in creating and agreeing the criteria for the target. They need to own it, have some control over it and personally commit to it. If you pick up any self-help book, appraisal model, counselling or coaching manual the message is the same. Students need to take responsibility for their own target setting and for monitoring progress against those targets. As part of classroom assessment, target setting can be genuinely useful to teachers and students but the targets must be owned by and meaningful to the student, connected to their wider aspirations and limited in number.

The huge emphasis on target setting and the bureaucracy that accompanies it irritates teachers. As more paperwork lands on our desks and in our inboxes we are inundated by demands for targets by senior managers who are, in turn, forced to spend a great deal of their time generating data. Targets for reports, behaviour, exams, literacy, numeracy, homework, coursework, attendance, healthy eating, breathing and being nice! It is a farcical bureaucratic paperchase that frustrates teachers who want to get on with teaching. At worst it is a bland and demotivating process that limits students' expectations and fuels the data trolls with a fetish for statistics, graphs and spreadsheets.

Whether the wider culture of target setting has actually improved education is not proven. In the classroom, however, effective target setting is an essential element of successful assessment. Get the emphasis right and you can see students using target setting to raise their own expectations and achievement.

'Target setting' is a phrase that has led many teachers to believe that they are responsible for setting targets for other people. When the emphasis is on teachers first setting the targets for their students and then working out the steps for the students to get there it is not a model that engages or supports autonomy. This model is also not compatible with Ofsted's drive for students to take ownership of their own learning. There is still a huge contradiction between what the inspectorate say about target setting in different contexts: in relation to classroom assessment the advice is to have shared targets that are student led and negotiated with teachers, yet in other published documents the advice is that it is most important that the targets *set* for each student are both realistic and challenging.

Teachers find themselves forced into generating targets that are not only meaningless for the students but are generated from stock responses. These stock responses might be generated automatically by software systems or from the target generator in our own heads: 'Jason's target is to try and act on all the targets he has been given while pretending that he is still an autonomous human being'. So many of us find ourselves paying lip service, playing a game that we know has little or no impact on achievement; jumping though hoops that are more about the paperchase than the student; more about the tickbox than the teaching.

Perhaps it is time to start questioning the received wisdom surrounding target setting. To devise a process that is owned by the students, to negotiate meaningful and useful targets, to limit the number of targets that an individual can reasonably be expected to hold, and to focus target setting on understanding the next step in learning as well as the dreams and aspirations of students.

Targets with an emotional kick

If target setting alone raised achievement our lives would be so much easier. We would be able to set a target, students would achieve it and then we could deliver another one. The truth is that when target setting raises achievement it does not do so in isolation.

Some people will keep targets predominantly in the rational brain. The target must be reached because the target has been set. For others the target needs an emotional attachment: 'I want to get my Maths GCSE/level 5 SAT/first class degree because my dad will be proud', 'I want to be able to structure sentences with more accuracy because I want to feel better about the way I come across to other people'. The emotional kick acts as a motivator. Without it there is little desire to work towards the target. The emotional connection is rarely highlighted. We know that human beings are led by their emotions. Targets that are framed solely with rational thought and references ignore the connections that really matter to the students.

Target setting only really has impact on achievement when:

- students really understand the detailed criteria that they are working towards;
- students take shared responsibility for setting the target;
- students monitor their own progress and record achievements towards the target;
- students are working on only two or three targets at any one time;
- students are motivated to work towards the targets – targets deal with the 'what' and the 'why', e.g. 'What is my target and why do I want to achieve it?', targets are matched with emotions, e.g. 'I want to be able to structure sentences with more accuracy because I want to feel better about the way I come across to other people';
- targets are meaningful, connected with the wider aspirations of the students.

> By the end of this lesson some of you will have learned what I planned to teach you, although some might not realise that they know it. Some of you will have learned entirely different things, about life or relationships. Others will wake up next week/month/year/century and be able to recall it but can not immediately answer the 'plenary' questions. →

> We spend a great deal of time trying to predict and categorise what students are going to learn when we actually have little control over it. Do the WALTs, WILTs and any number of funky ways to predict outcomes actually engage students, raise achievement or increase motivation to learn?
>
> For me, 'I am going to try and teach you something; when you think you have learned it let me know straight away', is a much more honest and intriguing proposition.

Strategy spotlight

Useful is more important than SMART

Smart targets look great and are organised, detailed, even seductive. It appears that everyone is on track, working diligently towards a definite goal, accountable for their performance and a fully paid up member of the 'society of correct learning'. The box is ticked, the management and inspectors are content and it seems that a rapid rise in achievement is inevitable.

For many teachers the term SMART has become a shorthand for 'not another huge bureaucracy'. Training days are organised, students are informed that they must all structure their targets in the same way. Those who have been successfully setting their own targets for years with their own methodology are shown a 'better way' and those who are just learning to think more strategically are forced into structures that demand too much too soon.

We differentiate and personalise our management of behaviour and teaching yet expect everyone to set targets in the same way. The truth is that some people find SMART targets extremely useful, while others are motivated and guided by targets that are not in the least SMART. Some people need to have their targets written down in triplicate, recorded and kept by their side at all times, while others hold their targets successfully in their heads. Targets work differently for different people. Personally I enjoy long-term, hard-to-measure, seemingly impossible and unrealistic targets. It is easy to assume that we all use targets in the same way and process them with similar language, but the truth is that it is as individual as our own fingerprint.

There may be a number of reasons why usually diligent teachers refuse to create SMART targets for students – they don't have time for the paperchase, they feel that setting targets for other people doesn't work or they don't buy into the SMART structure. The SMART structure is one way to do this but it can also be restrictive, long-winded and put people off. The importance of a target is that it is meaningful to the student. The fact that it doesn't fall into a particular system does not mean that it does not have an impact on achievement.

Useful targets are those that the student creates, drafts and commits to. How they are written or drawn is not as important as the meaning that they hold. Encourage them to be created using the students' own language and imagery, reinforce them using the students' own aspirations and emotions, map them clearly and resist limiting the timescales for them.

It is so much more important that the target is used than whether it is 'smart' or not.

Targets and expectations

'Schools/Colleges in which staff members collectively judge themselves capable of promoting academic success imbue their schools with a positive atmosphere for development that promotes academic attainments regardless of whether they serve predominantly advantaged or disadvantaged students.'

(Bandura, 1994)

The connection between high expectations and achievement and low expectations and failure is well documented. In Rosenthal and Jacobson's *Pygamlion in the Classroom* (1968), experiments students were given an IQ test to predict their achievement over the next academic year. The teachers were told which students would 'surge' forward and which students would not. In fact, the test scores were ignored and students were randomly grouped as 'surgers' and 'non-surgers'. Those identified as 'surgers' achieved significant improvements in standardised tests, those identified as 'non-surgers' did not. The expectations of the teachers had been the pivotal element.

After the assassination of Martin Luther King, Jane Elliot (see Going further, p. 93) tried to bring the realities of racism to her all-white class. She gave her pupils a pseudo-scientific explanation of how eye colour defined people that dramatically affected achievement. The brown-eyed students, she told them, were inferior to blue-eyed students. Brown-eyed students were described as untrustworthy, lazy and stupid, while blue-eyed students were given extra privileges. She segregated the two groups and made a point of praising the blue-eyed children and being negative to the brown. The transformation was dramatic. The blue-eyed children were bossy and derogatory towards their brown-eyed classmates. The brown-eyed students quickly became withdrawn, timid and defeated. Blue-eyed students improved their grades and were succeeding at tasks that had seemed out of reach before, while even the most gifted brown-eyed students stumbled over simple questions.

In *The Black and White Test Score Gap*, Jencks (1998) confirmed that race is an important part of the information teachers use to form an impression of a student and his or her potential. Simply put, when teachers expect students to do well and show intellectual growth, the students do so; when teachers do not have this expectation performance and growth are not as encouraged and may in fact be discouraged in a number of ways. We know this as the self-fulfilling prophecy and it plays havoc with target setting and assessment (see Figure 5.1).

The concept of the self-fulfilling prophecy

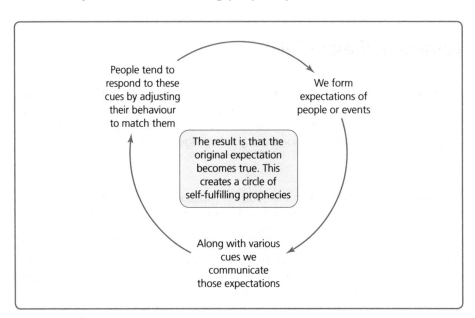

People tend to respond to these cues by adjusting their behaviour to match them

We form expectations of people or events

The result is that the original expectation becomes true. This creates a circle of self-fulfilling prophecies

Along with various cues we communicate those expectations

Figure 5.1

Students who are unable to set targets that will challenge themselves set easily attainable targets and expect themselves to fail, in a limiting self-fulfilling cycle. Students who are encouraged to reach further with their targets, set targets that stretch and expect themselves to achieve, and find that the self-fulfilling cycle boosts their achievement.

Students' expectations are easily set and not easily unpacked, so adjusting them is part of the skill of negotiating and structuring targets. Your expectations of the students are communicated in how you discuss targets with them. Spoon-feed targets to students and they get the idea that you think they can not think. If you deliberately structure target discussions you can help pitch expectations and leave the students with targets they own, even if some of them are guided by your own experience and knowledge of the student.

Target setting days

Target setting afternoons, days or meetings have become a popular way of developing target setting with students and their parents/mentors. When they are well structured, joined up and planned for they can be extremely productive. Unfortunately in many places the exercise has become devalued by its bureaucracy and the imposed workload. Subject teachers are given target sheets that they dutifully complete, often with no conversation with the student. The target sheets are passed to the form tutor. Some targets are refined, meaningful and useful. Others are generic, repetitive and, at worst, the same as targets that have been set for the rest of the group. As the students compare their reports they notice this and discuss it with their parents. At the meeting the tutor struggles to improvise a discussion around targets by pulling together strands from everyone else's targets. Often the targets come in late or are not clear and the tutor ends up making it up on the spot. Target setting meetings can work well but they rely on high-quality, negotiated targets being delivered in good time. If these meetings are important then time must be afforded for the planning and preparation.

Ideas for improving target setting discussions

'Goals that are not written down are just wishes.'

- Relax the conversation by diverting it.
- Empathise and build rapport.
- Word the targets using the student's language (not substituted by the 'proper word').
- Look for emotional hooks to link to targets.
- Reinforce what is going well and use this as a reason to raise expectations.
- Bring in the views of others/evidence/data gently with 'What do you think this is trying to say about you?'
- Hold up the mirror for the student with your questions.
- Take a 360-degree view – who is involved, who sees the targets, who else is invited to contribute to the discussion.
- Link the agreed targets to a set of images and agree where these are to be held.
- Agree any shorthand that you have used in the wording of the target. 'Accurate work means … ', 'Safe means … '.
- Help frame targets positively.

- Follow up, follow up!

- Question to increase motivation – ask 'What is stopping you from doing this immediately?'

- Make the students feel good about the conversation.

- Impose your own ideas when you have to and balance them with the ideas of the student.

- Assume that they have the answer and question them to find it.

- Summarise with the student by testing their recall of the discussion.

How many targets?

'Can I go home and get changed please, I am completely soaked in other people's targets.'

How many targets that you have set for yourself are you working towards? Write them down. Now write down all of the targets that other people have set for you. How many have you got? How many are you actively striving for? Split the targets into personal targets and work-related targets.

Now think of a student with average ability. How many work-related targets can they realistically hold and work with? As many as you have or less? Do you think the number of targets ought to be reduced according to age? How many of the targets will be cross-curricular and how many specific to a single subject area?

As a personal tutor expect to spend time protecting students from target overload. As well as negotiating and framing targets you will be shielding students from those trying to impose unnecessary and over-demanding targets. Those insisting on hijacking the students' priorities with their own must understand that there is a point at which more targets would be saturation.

Target sorting

If you recognise that your students are suffering from target overload then help them prioritise by asking the following:

- Which targets do you own?

- Which targets have been imposed on you?

- Which targets do you have a real motivation to achieve?

- Which targets have an emotional connection?

- Are you seeing common strands?

Having learners assist in defining goals increases the probability that they will understand them and want to reach them. However, students sometimes have unrealistic notions about what they can accomplish. Possibly they do not understand the precision with which a skill must be carried out or have the depth of knowledge to master some material. To identify realistic goals, we must be skilled in assessing a student's readiness or a student's progress toward goals.

Marking feedback

Feedback on students' work is often littered with arbitrary targets, such as 'You need to make all of this clearer' or 'Try to be more accurate here', and criteria-related targets that are not fully explained – 'This is not C grade work', etc. How do you make targets relevant to students when you are doing a summative assessment of work away from the student? How do you encourage students to respond to your marking without having to spend time with all of them? Try the following ideas:

- Focus in on the question rather than trying to provide the solution.

- Leave space for the student to respond to your comments – provide a simple hand stamp with a grid or sticky note that they can return to you.

- Follow the 3:1 rule – three positive aspects balanced with one constructive criticism.

- Be specific about how aspects of the work relate to the assessment criteria – 'This sentence really hits the mark, it is reflective and gives clear supporting arguments' is a long way from 'Great, love this!', etc.

- Reinforce your relationship with the student through meaningful and appropriate praise.

- Use the students' first names in written feedback.

Reflecting on practice

Don't write your target down ... draw it

Leading a training day on the day before everyone goes on holiday for Christmas is a tough gig. The minds of delegates are invariably awash with the pleasures, strains and plans for the days to come. You can see it in their eyes when they walk in and see it in their step as they walk out. Transferring skills learned on 22 December to the class you see again on 4 and 5 January takes more than good intentions. If a target is to be carried over and kept alive it needs to be embedded in the memory and recalled with

→

ease. To embed the target we created using the delegates' language, connect it to an image and display it discreetly.

Returning to a school where I had led training over a year before I was gently accosted by a smiling face on my return. Leading me to his room he reminded me of the target cards on which delegates had recorded targets last Christmas. (I had insisted that everyone write down their targets and posted them back to them in the new year.) Some had hurriedly made a note, most had doodled alongside with wintry themes, whereas he had drawn four icons that were posted by the side of his desk. They served as a clear reminder of the targets he had set himself in light of the training, could not be re-interpreted by the students and had clearly been there for over a year. He had found a way to discreetly but publicly display his own targets that was instantly transferrable to target setting with students.

Practical strategies for primary, secondary and further education

Primary

Special mission cards

Figure 5.2A: An example of Challenge Cards used at KS3 to encourage self study

Source: Special mission card idea and text courtesy of Karen Brown

WRITING CHALLENGES CARD 3 OF 7
(KEY VERRBS: CONCLUDE, INTERPRET, DISCRIMINATE)

✴ Experiment with writing in different genres

✴ Start your own list of 'WOW Words' (long, complicated and exciting new
  words to Wow your teachers)

✴ Write a five-scene drama script based on a current social issue

✴ Write an evaluative essay on a theatrical performance

✴ At home, practise mind-mapping plots for stories

  Cast iron guarantee!

  Your efforts have earned you a 24-hour turnaround guarantee
  on any extra work you submit

Figure 5.2B: The reverse of the card.

Source: Special mission card idea and text courtesy of Karen Brown

Secondary

Target analysis

Post up all of the targets set by a parallel group (without names) and ask your class to discuss them. Which targets are difficult to understand? Which seem too easy, too hard? Can you order the targets, create a ladder from them? Find an example of a well-written target. Are there targets that relate to certain levels or grades?

Students can then use the lists, discussion and reflection to inform how they structure and word their own targets.

Target maps

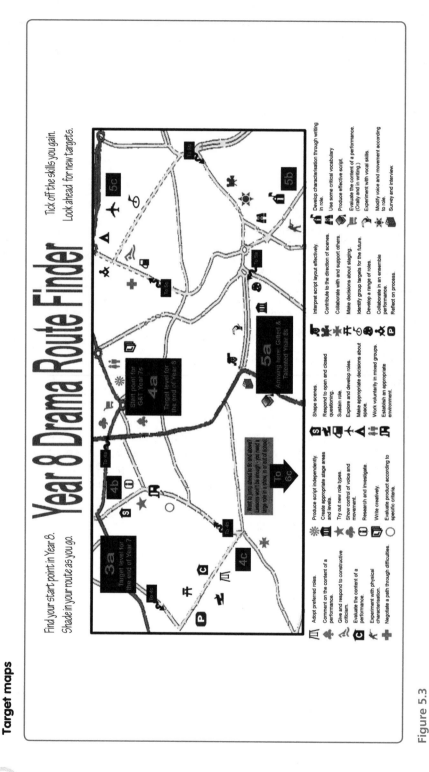

Figure 5.3

Source: Copyright © Karen Brown 2009. Reproduced with permission

Involve parents

Attach targets written by the students to school reports, send summaries of targets alongside a brief description of the work at regular intervals and send them the questions that they are likely to be asked during target meetings in advance. Let parents know when targets have been achieved, not only when promises are broken.

Further education/post-16

Visible targets

Post targets where they will be seen: in diaries, as daily reminders on digital calenders and mail programmes, as bookmarks, laminated cards on tables, screen savers on computers, wallpaper on mobile phones or on a sticker on the back of college ID cards.

Targeting grade discriminators

Ask students to mark a copy of their own work in preparation for a tutorial focused on reaching the next grade boundary. Compare their marked script with your marking and reference the grade descriptors or examiners guidelines. Target the discriminators between the grades or levels, the student's understanding of the criteria and their perception of what they need to do to reach it.

Exercise

Copy the table and follow the instructions below.

Priority	Target	Rational	Emotional

Write down your own professional and personal targets in column 2.

Now describe the rational reason for each target in column 3.

Now in column 1 give them a priority order.

Finally describe the emotional connection in column 4.

Look again at the priority order; do you want to make any changes?

Reflection

How many of your own targets are personal?

How many professional?

How much impact does emotion play in the prioritisation of your targets?

Could you use the grid with students to discuss similar issues?

Critical questions

- How do your students hold their targets and keep them fresh every day?

- How can you refresh your expectations of students through target setting?

- How can you restructure your target setting meetings so the student leaves owning the target?

- When is the next opportunity for you to share the way that you design, plan, create, revise and hold your own targets?

Conclusion

Improving the way that targets are negotiated is at the very core of successful assessment. Students who can see the other side of the river know which stepping stones they are going to take to get there. They know the skills, attitudes and knowledge they need to make the leaps. They hold their targets close. If your students rely on you to set their targets the shift in responsibility and autonomy is not complete. The way that we speak to students about their learning is affected by our own expectations of them. Without being conscious of it our language is littered with preconceptions, perceptions and unspoken labels.

Key ideas summary

- To motivate people to strive to achieve a target they need to be fully involved.

- Target setting at the task level is an essential element of successful classroom assessment.

- 'Target setting' is a phrase that has led many teachers to believe that they are responsible for setting targets for other people.

- The emotional kick acts as a motivator. Without it there is little desire to work towards the target.

- It is so much more important that the target is used than whether it is 'SMART' or not.

- Students' expectations are easily set and not easily unpacked. Adjusting them is part of the skills of negotiating and structuring targets.

- If a target is to be carried over and kept alive it needs to be embedded in the memory and recalled with ease.

Going further

Brown Eyes, Blue Eyes: www.janeelliott.com/

Rosenthal, R. and Jacobson, L. (1968) *Pygmalion in the Classroom*, Crown House Publishing

Jencks, C. (1998) *The Black and White Test Score Gap*, Brookings Institution Press.

How far have we come?

The assessment tree

New growth stretches further from the centre with a direction and a purpose. Students are controlling their direction, rate of gowth and pace of change.

Pivotal's Negotiated Assessment Grids (NAGs)

What this chapter will explore:

- A simple, flexible process for student assessment at the task level
- Using negotiated criteria to clarify understanding and promote target setting
- How to reduce your target setting paperwork and give students more responsibility

'Young children's potential for learning is vastly beyond what even teachers with high expectations believe.'

(Ted Wragg)

The Negotiated Assessment Grid (NAG), firmly based in educational theories and successful classroom practice, has far-reaching possibilities. It's not rocket engineering, it's more a synthesis of what we all do already but brought in to a clear and usable conceptual framework and method.

Pivotal's Negotiated Assessment model (see Going further, p. 107) is a highly flexible framework for classroom assessment and target setting at the task level. In a simple framework it encourages autonomy and responsibility for learning in the classroom, with students setting, monitoring and evaluating their own work and that of others. The model creates opportunities for self-, peer, group and teacher assessment and can be effortlessly adapted for all areas of the curriculum. It reduces preparation time for the teacher and is used to manage behaviour as well as learning.

'Pivotal's Assessment model makes what we have to do human.'

(Jonothan Neelands, Senior Lecturer in Drama Education, Warwick University)

At the core of this model for assessment is a simple grid. Drawn on paper or projected on the board, it frames the ideas and defines the negotiated agreement. There is nothing flash or difficult here. It is flexible enough to be used in any subject and with any age group. It is quickly understood and easily owned by the students.

The first and perhaps most obvious application for the NAG is in defining success criteria to assess skills. The initial frame for the question focuses the class. It forces them to imagine a successful outcome, like the 100-metre sprinter who sees him- or herself on the podium.

Imagine that you were reading an A grade design and technology paper …

If you were watching a great presenter and were utterly engaged in her …

What makes a successful … ?

What are the elements of an A grade … ?

What makes a believable … ?

What are the exact … ?

The question must elicit accurate, focused success criteria. Note it in the first column of the grid using the student's own language. A vital part of the process of negotiating criteria with the students is an acceptance of the language they use. It will be tempting to substitute their language for the subject specific language or with more academic terms. For some of us this correction of language is habitual. We do it without thinking as we try to encourage students to use a wider and more appropriate vocabulary. By accepting the students' own language we accept the way their knowledge and the way they think, link it clearly to the work and so engage them immediately in the work. We foster their autonomy even in the preliminary stages of setting up the grid.

'There can be no alternative in the initial stages to total acceptance of the language that the children bring with them.'

(Britton, 1970)

Why not try this?

When the criteria are established, make a point of reflecting the ideas back to the students with questions such as 'Whose ideas are these?' Students will slowly respond with, 'They're ours', and begin to realise that you are passing responsibility to them. Some may even sit forward in their chairs. It is also useful here to pull out your own list of criteria for this task and demonstrate to them that they have almost all of the criteria that you had listed, albeit using slightly different language: 'So if I am supposed to be the expert in this and you have chosen the same criteria what does this say about you? ... 'Yes, you are intelligent. I have been teaching this for 2/8/28 years and you seem to know exactly what is required.' Develop their engagement by reinforcing the knowledge and understanding that they bring to the task. Raise expectations by convincing them that they should have confidence in this work, after all they have already established the same criteria as a fully qualified teacher! This is particularly pertinent for those students with poor writing skills or your Year 8 boys who would rather wriggle than write. Use the grid as a vehicle for praising oral contributions which are often high-level ideas without the specific language.

'Whose ideas are these? Yes they are yours. Now you know that I am an experienced actor (*Holby*, *The Bill*, *DIY SOS*) and when I was preparing this lesson I missed a few of the criteria you have set. You are very good. You might also like to know that the GCSE board has a number of the criteria you have set.'

Now that you have the criteria, established groups and individuals can select criteria to place on their grids. It is this criteria that will be focused on during the task to the exclusion of all others. The teacher's responsibility is to tour the room, adjusting criteria selection and making sure that students are challenged but not setting themselves up to fail. Further engagement is created as groups start to negotiate with their peers and with their teacher.

Through this process you have successfully clarified the key vocabulary and learning objectives while differentiating for all abilities. In the corner of the room you can see a nervous smile from the Ofsted inspector, who lurks with an 'I'm not sure I can cover all of that with the limited number of tickboxes I have' look on his or her face.

So, with their minds organised, yet jam packed with ideas about how they can succeed in this lesson, the students rush off to their task. Is the NAG now dead? Not in the least. Both you and the students can use it further.

Staying 'on task' with the NAG

During the task students can be keeping their own and their groups' work focused by referring to the NAG to gauge their successes and target areas for improvement. Leave the grid by the side of the working area and they will naturally use it as an aide memoire for the task and the language they are practising. They may add points to their NAG, aiding teacher/student and student/student conversation or begin to develop the detailed language on the grid in preparation for a written task. Less confident groups enjoy the structure, challenging groups are reminded of their responsibilities and more able groups relish the independence. Eventually all students will be able to enter the room, find out what the task is and start to create their own grid.

The teacher can watch work in progress and then lead the group reflection using the students' ideas. Often during these conversations between student and teacher, if other students will clamour for your attention, simply refer to the NAG, ask the students to see if the answer to their query is on there, and let them know that you will be with them soon. Your role in the room changes. Rather than leading the assessment from the front, you are a roving expert, delivering guidance when and where it is needed.

During this phase, both students and teachers have been using the NAG as a vehicle to praise success and progress, and to set targets for future successes. As the grid fills up ideas and reflections from the oral process are held. You have deftly created a written record of the process without the 'Do we *have* to do written work?' argument.

The initial trials with the NAGs resulted in a great deal of evidence being recorded on large sheets of paper or on the board; not the easiest medium for collating evidence or developing comparative assessment data over time. In order to streamline the emerging assessment procedures and ensure we were not creating a system that burdened teachers with more paperwork it was essential to give the responsibility for the NAGs over to the students completely.

Early in the year, students are guided towards a stack of blank NAGs, which can be used by groups and individuals for assessed tasks. Often the NAG is a blend of teacher-directed criteria for individuals or groups, but students have responsibility for completing the pro forma and storing the evidence. Students grab a blank NAG at the beginning of an assessed task, tailoring it for the activity. As their familiarity with the system increases they strive to use appropriate language and subject specific terminology. Their paired peer assessment becomes particularly good and the problem of being able to assess large groups of performers at one time is solved. At times the targets which come from the reflection at the end of one session can slot straight into the next NAG and so individual target setting at the task level with large groups of 'untrained' students is completed with no additional paperwork for the teacher.

Negotiated Assessment formalises that which is at the core of good teaching: creating frameworks that allow the students to take control of their own learning, deconstructing tasks and skills, and empowering students to succeed as reflective autonomous learners.

Use the checklist (or grid) below in different ways:

- Give each group a copy of the checklist to place in their working area. As the group works the teacher provides written feedback in the second column. Students can then choose when to stop, examine and respond to this. Praise and criticism are discreet and personalised. You can comment in words, symbols or agreed numbers and grades.

- To record self-reflection and self-evaluation against the criteria (column 3).

- As a framework for students engaged in a focused peer assessment. Feedback given as written notes in column 4 – three comments on what is going well earns the right to one criticism

- As a place to record and hold teacher and LSA comments, questions, reinforcement and guidance.

What makes a believable/good/A grade/precise ....?

	Teacher assessment	Self-assessment	Peer assessment	Target(s)
(Teacher's choice)				
(Teacher's choice)				

Now use the completed grid to:

- Highlight key vocabulary.

- As an aide memoire to support written work/homework, e.g. 'Can you record the activity that we have done and evaluate your contribution to its success?'

- To create a marking scheme.

- As a rolling record of criteria that relates to a particular examination/target – on the wall of the teaching space or as part of teacher/student record keeping.

- Compare success criteria with that published by the examining board.

Here is an example of a grid used for teaching presentation skills with Year 8 working in pairs:

Sample Negotiated Assessment Grid

Name: **Class:**   **Date:**

What are the precise skills for effective presentation?

What we are learning to do?	Success criteria	How was this achieved?	Self-reflection	Agreed targets
Improve vocal skills	Use emphasis and pause to help communicate meaning Vary speed appropriately Vary volume appropriately			
Develop skills in presentation	Clear, appropriate use of gesture Expressive use of space Communication of status			
Work effectively in groups	Collaborate to complete a group performance Complete delegated tasks			

What educational purpose does a NAG serve?

- Literacy across the curriculum.
- Metacognition for learners.
- Opportunities to praise.
- Opportunities for students to set targets.
- A system for developing autonomous learners.
- Information for creating an evidence base.
- Teacher target setting.
- Oracy to literacy.
- Self-, peer and teacher assessment at the task level and beyond.
- Assessment that can be observed.

How does the NAG satisfy QCDA's Ten Principles of Assessment for Learning?

The QCDA requirement	The 'You should…'	Does the NAG satisfy the criteria? Y/N
Assessment for learning should be part of effective planning of teaching and learning	A teacher's planning should provide opportunities for both learner and teacher to obtain and use information about progress towards learning goals. Planning should include strategies to ensure that learners understand the goals they are pursuing and the criteria that will be applied in assessing their work.	
Assessment for learning should focus on how students learn	The process of learning has to be in the minds of both learner and teacher when assessment is planned and when the evidence is interpreted. Learners should become as aware of the 'how' of their learning as they are of the 'what'.	

→

The QCDA requirement	The 'You should…'	Does the NAG satisfy the criteria? Y/N
Assessment for learning should be recognised as central to classroom practice	Assessment processes are an essential part of everyday classroom practice and involve both teachers and learners in reflection, dialogue and decision making.	
Assessment for learning should be regarded as a key professional skill for teachers	Teachers require the professional knowledge and skills to plan for assessment, observe learning, analyse and interpret evidence of learning, give feedback to learners and support learners in self-assessment.	
Assessment for learning should be sensitive and constructive because any assessment has an emotional impact	Teachers should be aware of the impact that comments, marks and grades can have on learners' confidence and enthusiasm and should be as constructive as possible in the feedback that they give.	
Assessment for learning should take account of the importance of learner motivation	Motivation can be preserved and enhanced by assessment methods which protect the learner's autonomy, provide some choice and constructive feedback, and create opportunity for self-direction.	
Assessment for learning should promote commitment to learning goals and a shared understanding of the criteria by which they are assessed	For effective learning to take place learners need to understand what it is they are trying to achieve – and want to achieve it. Understanding and commitment follows when learners have some part in deciding goals and identifying criteria for assessing progress.	
Learners should receive constructive guidance about how to improve	Learners need information and guidance in order to plan the next steps in their learning. Teachers should: • pinpoint the learner's strengths and advise on how to develop them; • be clear and constructive about any weaknesses and how they might be addressed; • provide opportunities for learners to improve upon their work.	

→

The QCDA requirement	The 'You should…'	Does the NAG satisfy the criteria? Y/N
Assessment for learning develops learners' capacity for self-assessment so that they can become reflective and self-managing	Independent learners have the ability to seek out and gain new skills, new knowledge and new understandings. They are able to engage in self-reflection and to identify the next steps in their learning. Teachers should equip learners with the desire and the capacity to take charge of their learning through developing the skills of self-assessment.	
Assessment for learning should recognise the full range of achievements of all learners	Assessment for learning should be used to enhance all learners' opportunities to learn in all areas of educational activity. It should enable all learners to achieve their best and to have their efforts recognised.	

Source: Adapted from 'The 10 Principles: Assessment for Learning', QCDA (www.qcda. gov.uk/4336.aspx). Reproduced with permission

Supporting students as they experiment with new language and new linguistic structures

If you want to ensure productive conversations about learning then you need to teach the skills and attitudes that you want to see and hear. Teachers often bemoan the lack of speaking and listening skills that students have but how many of us see it as our responsibility to teach and develop them? Fortunately there are practical strategies that are simple to implement, highly effective and make a long-term impact on the quality of conversations that surround learning and assessment.

As the quality of the speaking and listening work rises so the quality of feedback improves. Other teachers walking past your room will catch snippets of conversations that surprise and amaze. Students enjoy learning new language and playing with structures and in turn this is reflected in their writing.

I have lost count of the number of lessons I have observed where key terminology is introduced at the beginning and then not referred to at the end of the lesson. Language teachers know that to develop language use students need to practise, to speak the words out loud and then use them independently in the correct context. In many classrooms the key words are posted up as if putting them on the board was enough.

If you want students to integrate the language into their vocabulary, or to be comfortable using more advanced sentence structures, a framework for speaking is invaluable. Teachers have been using writing frames to support writing for many years. Translate this idea to speaking and oracy frames to make absolute sense.

> 'The connection between thought and word ... is neither preformed nor constant. It emerges in the course of development, and itself evolves. To the biblical "In the beginning was the Word", Goethe makes Faust reply, "In the beginning was the deed". The intent here is not to detract from the value of the word, but we can accept this version if we emphasize it differently: In the beginning was the deed. The word was not the beginning – action was there first; it is the end of development, crowning the deed.'

> (Vygotsky, 1962)

Extending conversations through oracy frames

'From thought to word to the page!'

When students have frameworks to lead their speech they feel supported enough to take a risk. They experience delivering the extended language that you expect. In time, extended thought and speech will become more natural, and an expected part of classroom conversation.

Students who are not practised in developing conversations beyond single phrases or who say as little as possible or who give stock responses need supporting. Oracy frames are negotiated and agreed frameworks for feedback. If they are designed well they guide students to speak in sentences, organising thoughts and integrating subject specific language.

You might choose to set parameters, e.g. 'Three sentences each', or agree time limits for the conversation, e.g. 'OK, you have 45 seconds to discuss the first area that needs improvement'. You could also direct the conversation, e.g. 'You must reply with an extended sentence that ends in a question', or ask a question from four of the question cue categories.

Some examples for maths

Discussion in maths

Why speaking and listening in maths? To develop understanding, to track the thought processes and identify correct paths, to identify the people who are following the process but don't have the comprehension – we need to understand that they understand. Students need to be able to demonstrate their understanding.

What structures are useful?

John's answer is … , I noticed that he … .

We want to know … , the way we find this out is … .

I got the wrong answer because … .

The accuracy is …

I can prove … by using the method … .

I recognise the pattern … , it reminds me of … .

I know this is the right answer because … .

I got the answer by … , but I could have got the answer by doing … too.

I have collected data about … and I have determined that it demonstrates … .

Key words (tick each time you use one)

Product	Sum	Total	Equation	Fraction	Percentage
☐ ☐ ☐	☐ ☐ ☐	☐ ☐ ☐	☐ ☐ ☐	☐ ☐ ☐	☐ ☐ ☐

Bonus words

Denominator	Numerator	Negative	Infinity	Decimal	Proof
☐ ☐ ☐	☐ ☐ ☐	☐ ☐ ☐	☐ ☐ ☐	☐ ☐ ☐	☐ ☐ ☐

Exercise

Collect subject-specific sentence stems and extenders, together with key words and extended vocabulary to create your own oracy frame. You might design this for a specific topic or as a generic aide memoire for feedback.

Design your own oracy frame

Key words (Tick each time you use one)

…………	…………	…………	…………	…………	…………
☐ ☐ ☐	☐ ☐ ☐	☐ ☐ ☐	☐ ☐ ☐	☐ ☐ ☐	☐ ☐ ☐

Bonus words

…………	…………	…………	…………	…………	…………
☐ ☐ ☐	☐ ☐ ☐	☐ ☐ ☐	☐ ☐ ☐	☐ ☐ ☐	☐ ☐ ☐

For further material available for download on sentence stems, visit www.pearsoned.co.uk/essentialguides.

Conclusion

The NAG encourages the teaching style that rigorous student-led assessment demands. There are worthwhile risks that need to be taken and then taken again until the students accept responsibility for their own learning. The NAG works as well with analogue teaching (large sheets of paper and thick pens) as it does with new technology. The grids are stored, reviewed and owned by the students. Whether they are written, typed or drawn it is the process of negotiation and independent target setting at the task level that is so important.

Key ideas summary

- The first and perhaps most obvious application for the NAG is in defining success criteria to assess skills.

- Focus the question to elicit that it is pertinent to the task.

- Use the student's language in the first instance and on the grid.

- Reflect back the achievements of the students as you develop the grid with them. Make them feel that they own the ideas and the work.

- Students can keep their own and their group's work focused by referring to the NAG to gauge their successes and target areas for improvement.

- The role of the teacher changes when students own the process, the criteria and take responsibility for driving their own work.

- Use the completed grids as evidence of work, target setting, log of contributions and ideas, as a rolling record of achievement.

Going further

Negotiated Assessment Grid, www.pivotaleducation.com/assessment.php

How far have we come?

The assessment tree

The NAGs encourage growth and understanding in all directions. New learning is recorded, mapped and assessed. The teacher prunes the new growth predicting which shoots will eventually bear fruit.

Managing active assessment in the classroom

What this chapter will explore:

- Strategies for managing changes in behaviour as assessment processes become more student-led
- Your changing role as a teacher
- How to ensure group work is productive, meaningful and focused

'In all chaos there is a cosmos, in all disorder a secret order.'

(Carl Jung)

With more active classrooms and more responsibility given to the students there will be different challenges for the management of behaviour. As the students embed the new processes this chapter gives the teacher guidance on how to manage the behaviours that will change and new behaviours that will emerge.

It is often assumed that the more active the task the more difficult it will be to manage behaviour. It is why I so often see classes who are not allowed to do more than complete worksheets, with their teachers complaining that 'I can't do anything else with them'. In fact the reverse is often true. Students who are forced to sit at their desks and complete uninspiring generic activities are often those who actively seek to undermine their teachers and subvert the task. With risk there are dangers but there are also rewards. Students who are given responsibility and autonomy become motivated and engaged to work on a task in a way that worksheets can never do.

I remember an NQT asking to observe a lesson that was active with students who were challenging so that she could take away some ideas for her own group. I sent her to see a food technology teacher working with a notorious Year 11 group. A master in subtle management of even the trickiest students, the teacher was one of the best in the school. The NQT returned from the lesson and I asked her what she had learned. 'Nothing,' came the reply, 'there was no bad behaviour, no swearing, no defiance, not even a fist fight!' She was clearly disappointed that there was no obvious inappropriate behaviour. I suspected that the skills of the teacher were so covert that they had been impossible to observe. The following week I accompanied her to the same lesson so that we might observe together.

As the teaching commenced I was able to point out to the NQT the preventive strategies that the teacher employed to divert students away from inappropriate behaviour. Together we noted the non-verbal nudges, gentle positive reinforcement, skilled positioning and movement around the room, changes of pace, shifts in tone and gentle manipulation of language.

This kind of focused paired observation helps to show that managing an active classroom is not about one big idea or one way of working. It is about keeping one step ahead of the students and using a range of techniques that allow risk. Those who are most practised at it have skills that are difficult to spot with the naked eye.

Routines, routines, routines

The successfully active classroom might look chaotic but it demands structure. Organisational, teaching and learning routines must be negotiated, taught, displayed and constantly reinforced. It is through routines that the most active classrooms run efficiently and seamlessly. Too often we assume students already know how to behave. Relentlessly teaching through agreed routines does not leave room for this assumption. The success of active tasks is not left to chance.

Embedding new routines needs more commitment than posting up a sheet of A4 behind your desk. This is not about setting a routine but agreeing it and then teaching it through consistent and persistent positive reinforcement. Too often new routines are used as a stick with which to 'beat' the students. To teach routines well a shift of attention is needed, not so that inappropriate behaviour is ignored but so students who are following the agreement are 'caught' doing so. This interaction also gives you an opportunity to reinforce the expectations for others: 'Great, you are giving really focused and relevant feedback using the criteria we agreed', is so much more effective than 'Why oh why are you still talking about the football?', etc.

Your own routines also need attention.

Thirty days to change a habit

Many teachers, keen to experiment with more active and risky teaching strategies, dive in, get burned and then run back to the comfort of worksheet land. The truth is that to change the expectations and habits of your students takes more than one well-planned lesson. To create sustainable change needs at least 30 days.

Consider how you change your own habits. If you have given up smoking you know that after a week it is easy and tempting to fall off the wagon. After two weeks you no longer wake up in the morning thinking of cigarettes, after three you can eat a meal without craving one immediately afterwards and after four weeks the routine has been changed so much that you can go days without thinking of the weed. The problem with changing habits, and particularly those you enjoy, is that thinking about changing them forever can make the first steps seem unattractive. Never having another cigarette, another drink or designing another worksheet seems like a tall order; our instinct is to maintain the habit as the thought of never doing it again is unattractive. To commit to changing a routine or habit for 30 days is less onerous and will make it so much easier to make a decision to change for the long term.

If you find yourself reluctant to take a risk, worried about making learning more active or nervous about changing established processes for classroom assessment, then make a commitment just for 30 days. At the end of the 30 days you can return to your old practice if you find that no improvements are discernible. Perhaps, however, you may wake up in the second week and not reach for the worksheet.

Knowing when not to negotiate

Negotiating rules and responsibilities with students sounds entirely sensible, democratic and downright decent. Students should feel empowered through their involvement in decision making, and so take more responsibility for their own actions. When you have built a good relationship with the group then the negotiation can be efficient and productive. Negotiating with classes with whom you have not developed a long-term relationship carries unforeseen dangers. Starting the first lesson with a new group of students with lengthy negotiations on expectations, rules and routines sends confusing messages to many of the students. Is their new teacher soft? Weak? Indecisive? Who is in charge? Is everything now negotiable? For now you are the teacher and you get to decide what the rules are. Holding clear and definite expectations for behaviour and learning sets a standard for the students to reach. Posting your rules on the wall is a simple assertive act that draws a clear line in the sand. There is no doubt about what the rules are and who has the ultimate responsibility in policing them. With a clear set of initial rules and 'starter' routines as a foundation you can decide the appropriate time to negotiate and rework.

Making agreements that stick

- Inviting contributions.
- Discussing from a draft template.
- Posting up alternatives and asking for a response over time.
- Involving students in the creation of the signs.
- Planning in opportunities to refer to the routines and reflect on their usefulness.
- Agreeing a time to review the routines.
- Moving on from routines once they are embedded.

Processes

Encouraging students to take responsibility for the process of classroom assessment inevitably means lots of bits of paper, or ideas recorded in different places and through different media. The process that you use comes with its own organisational challenges that if not well planned for can undermine the activity before it has begun. Involving students in the logistics as well as the content is an important part of them taking responsibility.

Embed the processes in the organisation of the classroom. The webs of ideas on the displays, the slips of paper to make checklists on, the peer assessment notebooks for each student, the criteria whiteboard to write up new ideas onto, key word ladder, great ideas tree, oracy frames designed as mobiles hanging from the ceiling …

Strategy spotlight

You are the most important practitioner

Modelling the task with students is a useful way to explain complex activities for the class; stepping into role yourself reveals much about your expectations and how a performance can be developed. Students value and appreciate teachers who can demonstrate their skill as a practitioner. If you are always in the role of director, they will have no role model for learning; many will find it difficult to see beyond the limits of their experience.

Your modelling is an essential part of your role as lead learner. The drama teacher who does not act, the PE teacher who won't run or a music teacher who won't play in front of others are all missing a trick. Your modelling is a risk that will pay off, it is central to the achievement of the groups that you teach.

Managing groups and their assessment

Students who are reluctant to peer assess

1. The student who does not want to show their work to others

- Reinforce the confidential nature of the assessment and highlight who will see it.

- Make them feel safe enough to take a risk in the classroom.

- Speak to them privately away from the lesson about your expectations for all students.

- Make specific agreements with them about what happens in a lesson when it is time for peer assessment. You might decide to give them a get-out pass that can be used once per half term or negotiate working partners with them.

2. Disagreements within working groups

- Refocus the whole group on the task and assessment criteria.

- Refer to the learning ritual.

- Move the group away from talking and back to practically working through an idea: 'There are two strong ideas here, you all need to take five to ten minutes to work through them, and then call me back if you need an objective opinion'.

- Encourage them to view such frustrations as a natural part of the creative process.

3. Groups who drift off-task

- Refer the group to the learning ritual.

- Apply warnings and then sanctions to those who choose not to follow the ritual.

- Support those who decide to follow the ritual with praise and positive reinforcement.

- Encourage the group to present or perform (to a small audience, not the whole class), even if they are under-rehearsed/prepared.

- Hold the group back after the lesson and explain your expectations clearly and what will happen in the next lesson if the behaviours are repeated.

TOP TIP!

Keeping groups 'on-task'

Draw up/agree a checklist of ten success criteria for students to work on. Number the working groups and as you notice different groups succeeding record their group number against the target. Students will start looking at the checklist, focusing on the skills for the task and try to get each one ticked off for their group. You will be able to identify and encourage groups who are having difficulty and better gauge if the time you have given them for the activity is appropriate. At the end of the preparation period each group will naturally refer back to the checklist. If the groups are presenting their work, the checklist can be used by the audience to give accurate feedback using appropriate terminology.

Too much too soon

We have all had the same experience: delivering detailed instructions and expectations for the task, only to find that the rest of the lesson is spent explaining it over to individual groups. Try limiting yourself to three instructions for the task in the first instance. You can then get students on to their feet and working quickly with a clear focus. As the lesson develops, you can stop the class using one group to model or workshop your next instructions. Limit your interjections to one minute and a maximum of two further instructions: 'I need your full attention for one minute to explain only two things'. The pace of the lesson can be enhanced by giving students a clear deadline for the new focus: 'You now have five minutes to create two critical moments and find an ending line'. In this way, students are able to maintain their focus on specific skills and techniques, you can remain flexible in your development of the task and your time is spent teaching and creating, not firefighting.

Practical strategies for primary, secondary and further education

Primary

Ball of string

In large open teaching areas defining spaces for groups to work in is vital. As you allocate groups their working area give each group a length of string. The string is used to define the working area. Spotting students who leave their own group becomes easier and arguments about who owns which space are eliminated. As well as a useful strategy for managing group work you can use it to explore the following:

- *Proxemics* – severely limit the performance space with working in small circles.

- *Staging* – suggest different shapes for the students to work in, with different audience configurations.

- *Differentiation* – asking all students to work to the limits of their performance area with more able students given longer lengths.

Secondary

Transformers

The hassle of moving the furniture around stops many teachers from experimenting with more active approaches. Try establishing a strict routine for moving the room into different configurations. Consider splitting the group into competing teams or drilling selected students to take responsibility. Take some time to make sure that they can switch between configurations quickly, safely and accurately. Once perfected you can change your room in a matter of seconds, impress inspectors, amaze visitors and choose your configuration to suit your lesson rather than the other way around.

Further education/post-16

Student assessors

Promote the role of student assessors by introducing training, grading and rewarding of skilled assessment. Define the skills of good assessors as criteria and graduate levels so that students see the progression. Perhaps only assessors will have to reach the highest grade in order to pre-mark coursework or monitor the target setting of others.

Reflecting on practice

The best-laid plans of mice and insurance executives!

One of the first training days that I led was a team-building event for a large insurance company. I thought that the corporate world was ready for some new ideas from education and that I was the man to deliver it. I may have been new to the business but I was shocked to discover how little even the most senior managers for an international business understood about managing and motivating people. I found that the approach to assessment and peer feedback in the workplace was entirely focused on what was wrong, what the mistakes were. The delegates had clearly made a career out of managing other people very badly.

The exercise in which we were engaged was very simple. A team of eight people lift a team member above their heads while the group who are watching observe what they are doing to see that it is correct. I introduced the 3:1 idea and asked them to make sure that they were ready to give feedback on the positive aspects of the lift. The team who were lifting demonstrated their lift and I turned to the watching group, saying 'Can you tell me what you saw that demonstrated safe lifting?' The responses came thick ➡

and fast: 'Well, he is so fat that he can't bend down' and 'Did you see his little arms struggling to reach' and even 'I could nearly see up her skirt'. But for the suits and middle age paunches, I might have easily been in a Year 9 class! This group of managers either hadn't been to the equality and diversity training, or more likely they giggled all the way through it.

I gently reminded the group that we were looking for what was going well, what was successful, and set up the group who were demonstrating again. Again they performed their lift and again I turned to the audience and asked them for examples of what was good. 'They nearly dropped her on her head, that was rubbish', and 'They didn't have the right people in the right places', and even 'Now I can see down her top!'

You might imagine that this group of well-paid executives had been on every course, read every management book and studied the psychology of management into the early hours. However, they were unable to see what was going well before they had exhausted themselves in attacking each other about what was wrong. Even after being reminded, cajoled and encouraged to reflect on what was going well they were unable to do it. Their habits were firmly established and very difficult to untangle. They had gone further than simply being lazy about feedback. They had crossed over into a darker place. Their critical outlook had led to teasing and mild bullying as the way they interacted with each other. There was no space left for encouragement, enjoyment in success or enthusiasm for learning.

In the classroom groups of students can find themselves in the same predicament. Their communication is dominated by teasing: 'Your mum...', 'You are a study boy!' etc. Whereas changing the habits of successful managers is an uphill struggle, students are more malleable and their habits can be changed more easily.

The students before us today are the management of tomorrow – I know the managers that I would prefer to work for.

Exercise

As a starting point for a discussion with students, draft a routine for one of the following:

- Peer assessment for marking written work.
- Group discussion that affords everyone an equal voice.
- Moving furniture quickly and safely.
- Group assessment that balances positive reinforcement with a critical eye.

→

1.

2.

3.

4.

5.

Critical questions

- Are you designing lessons to fit the configuration of your room or configurations to fit lessons?

- Are you waiting for behaviour to change before you take a risk in a more active approach?

- Could a more active approach to assessment engage more students and actually ease disruptive behaviour?

Conclusion

As you introduce new strategies the behaviour of students will change. The behaviour of students can not be allowed to restrict the amount of responsibility you give or dictate your approach to assessment. It takes time and effort to change the expectations, habits and routines of students who join your class. It is your commitment to achieving a genuinely successful classroom assessment that is critical. This perseverance will, in time, change the behaviours and expectations that students bring.

Key ideas summary

- Active assessment changes behaviour; plan for the changes and take a risk.
- Embed routines that are agreed, displayed and constantly reinforced.
- Set clear expectations for group work.
- Aim to change habits over 30 days, not overnight.

Going further

Dix, P. (2007) *The Essential Guide to Taking Care of Behaviour*, Longman.

You can sign up for free tips on managing behaviour in the active classroom at www.pivotaleducation.com.

How far have we come?

The assessment tree

The pace of growth increases and the tree must be well managed and carefully shaped. Independent choice must be balanced with the needs of the group.

Differentiation and personalisation of assessment

What this chapter will explore:

- Strategies for ensuring that classroom assessment works for your most able students as it does for those who are struggling and those who find themselves somewhere in-between
- Using personal profiles so that students regularly check their progress against agreed criteria
- How to integrate students' self-assessment into summative reporting

'Perhaps a lunatic was simply minority of one.'

(George Orwell)

Classroom assessment that is personalised and differentiated is not an impossible dream! Yet with so many students passing through the hands of the average class teacher, truly personalised learning can not be the sole responsibility of the adults. It must be shared with the students. Teach your students how to differentiate for themselves while creating a simple coding for your schemes of work and you can satisfy both students and inspectors. Using classroom assessment to personalise learning for and with the students sounds like a tall order. In reality it can save you time, suit your planning and give you more time for monitoring and guiding learning.

Institutions are desperately trying new organisational structures in order to personalise learning. From Vertical Tutoring to house structures to learning communities, changing the system is seen as key. The truth is that the size of most classes in maintained schools and colleges perpetually works against an individual or personal approach. Even the most old school teachers in traditional independent schools are able to take a more personal view of learning because they have more time to spend with each student. They can spend more time with them due to the luxury of smaller class sizes. For the accountants and the politicians, reducing class size is discounted as being far too expensive. They would rather save money and bolt on policies; what they end up with is a sow's purse from a pig's ear.

Why not try this?

Simple criteria lists that students generate and then use to set their own objectives are quickly established and extremely useful. You can do this as a whole group or with individual students e.g. 'List the attributes of a good listener', 'How can we tell when a wall has been built by a craftsman?', 'What makes a good ending to a story?', 'What steps might we take when drafting a landscape design?' The question might be focused on the lesson content or on the conduct of students: 'What behaviours does the group need to show for a productive discussion?' Once the list has been established you can use it in many ways according to the age of the groups you are teaching. For younger children the list, posted on the wall, can be used to positively reinforce the behaviours that you want to see through the lesson. You might couple this with a class target: 'If you earn a tick/name/initials next to each of these criteria by the end of the lesson then we will be able to do that experiment that you really enjoy.' (The one where I always manage to blow myself up a little!) You might want to agree the criteria for good listening or group work and then catch students meeting the criteria.

With older students you might allow them to self-differentiate by encouraging them to choose two or three criteria that they are going to strive for in the next

5/10/20/50 minutes. Try asking individuals to suggest criteria for their partners or groups for one another. Students can record the criteria that they are working towards on a piece of paper that is placed on the desk next to where they are working. As you tour the classroom your feedback can be more precise and your assessment of work in progress concentrated on the chosen criteria. Differentiate by negotiating and redrawing criteria that are not set at an appropriate level.

Use the lists to prompt students who are drifting and reinforce those who are soaring. Use them as a rolling record of what has been accomplished, a model for other groups to examine, a standard for younger children to aspire to. Your role becomes one of the monitor, questioning some choices, helping to refine strategy with them. It takes you away from the 'this is what you should be doing' and into 'tell me what you have decided to do'. The shift of emphasis in assessment starts to build in choices that the student can use to personalise and differentiate.

How computer-generated assessment criteria works against the personalisation of assessment

The use of 'statement banks' to create summative reports flies in the face of efforts to personalise and individualise the assessment process. Generic comments that are carefully constructed to link with any number of additional generic comments mean that the final report appears to be individually crafted. In fact it could hardly be less personal. Levels have replaced grades and make little sense to most parents and employers, comments are generated by teachers with no input from the students, and the result is a report that is so impersonal all that has been changed is the name of the student. Students and parents busily comparing reports realise they have been conned when they see the duplication.

Computer-generated reports have not been introduced because it was thought that it would provide parents and students with more accurate information. The systems were bought in to save teachers time and face. The number of spelling mistakes and grammatical errors that appear when some teachers are asked for handwritten reports is shocking. Managers are certainly relieved that they no longer have to chase colleagues around with a bottle of Tippex and a list of linguistic crimes. Some teachers are relieved that they can save time by cutting and pasting without thinking (something that the same teachers would criticise their students for) and others thankful that they don't have to create new comments for each of the 130 students they teach. Summative reporting has been redesigned to meet the needs of the teachers. Personal touches, individual comments and genuine differentiation have been designed out.

The best reports are created with reasonable deadlines for completion. If it is genuinely important then time needs to be given for student comments, negotiated targets and focused thoughts of the teacher. They take time and effort. Certainly more effort than 'A2, C1, D5 and level 4'. We do ourselves a disservice by providing reports that have to be translated by the student and parent from computerised 'teacher speak'. As a profession we talk a great deal about the value of parental partnership, yet given a regular opportunity to communicate we shoot ourselves in the foot by overdesigning a system in the interests of the institution and not the home.

> ## TOP TIP!
>
> *Ask the students to write their own individual class report with evidence to back up the statements. Tell them that if you agree with their comments and they have strong evidence then you will use their comments as part of your reports. Each report will be evidence based, negotiated with students and their involvement will save you time.*

Personal assessment profiles

Personal profiles are an important part of the assessment process, giving students an opportunity to reflect back on what they have experienced and achieved over the term. They are required to give evidence of their best pieces of work in three categories and set themselves targets for future progress.

Profiles are best completed in the penultimate week of term, by which time the teacher should have a good understanding of appropriate levels for each student. The teacher levels are used at the end of the profiling session so that the student's level can be compared.

If a student feels their levels score in any area is too low, he or she should look again at the levels criteria for what they think should be their score – this criteria should be displayed in every teaching space so that large groups can all use the criteria at the same time. If, after comparing with the teacher's data, the student thinks that he or she has evidence of having achieved a higher level, he or she should discuss this privately with the teacher.

The teacher should not be afraid to listen carefully to the student's point and, where appropriate, either change the level score or help explain to the student why he or she might not be at that score yet. It is important that students do not expect to move onto the next level at each profiling session. The criteria that are displayed need to be detailed so that the levels/grades are broken down into sub-groups that show smaller steps. The emphasis must be on students identifying their own level/

grade according to the criteria and then providing supporting evidence for it. Students are in the best position to reflect back on learning.

Exercise

Personal profile

Name: **Group:**

Teacher: **Term:**

Writing   Previously I was on level ☐   My end of year level is ☐

Describe your best piece of written work this term:

....

....

Reading   Previously I was on level ☐   My end of year level is ☐

Describe your best piece of reading this term:

....

....

Speaking and listening   Previously I was on level ☐   My end of year level is ☐

Describe your best piece of speaking and listening performance this term:

....

....

My main achievement this term was: **My targets for next year are:**

1.

2.

3.

➡

Personal profile

The projects I have experienced this year were:

1. ....   4. ....

2. ....   5. ....

3. ....   6. ....

My **most successful** project was: ....

....

because: ....

....

....

My **least successful** project was: ....

....

because: ....

....

....

How have I made progress in **writing?**

How have I made progress in **reading?**

How have I made progress in **speaking and listening?**

Strategy spotlight

Has chalk and talk been replaced by screen and demean?

With new schools awash with ICT the organisation of the classroom often reverts back to students sitting in rows with the teacher's desk at the front. This is after all how the architects plan the sizes of classrooms when they build new schools. With the arrival of interactive whiteboards some classrooms are beginning to resemble mini lecture theatres. In most classrooms, PowerPoint is king. Lessons are planned and executed using this software, yet reading words and images from a screen is no more engaging than blackboards, chalk, OHP (overhead projectors), pens and flipcharts. Ask the children from the 50s, 60s, 70s and 80s what was similar about their schooling and they often talk of 'copying off the board'. Ask the children schooled in the last two decades what is consistent between teachers and it is likely to be staring at the PowerPoint presentation.

Both teacher and student are forced to spend a great deal, if not all, of the lesson staring at a screen. Both of whom for different reasons will have spent most of the previous evening staring at a screen. Eye contact and sometimes even personal contact is lost. The two hooded youths in the far corner hardly need to feel more isolated from society than they already do. The balance must be addressed.

Differentiating the environment

If you give students a choice over how they sit rather than just where they sit strange things happen. Some will immediately turn their chair around, others head for the floor, lying, sprawling or flexing into a meditative pose. Some will pace in straight lines, others walk in circles and some just sit. We arrange teaching spaces for many reasons: new theory on learning, our personal preference as a teacher, ability groupings, to keep everyone facing the board or to make sure that none can escape! How often do we include student preference in these decisions? We spend a great deal of time differentiating our content and significantly less in adjusting the environment so that it is more suited to the needs of the individual. I am not suggesting that we allow all of our students to lie around on the floor at a whim, but if the room is arranged to preclude any personal choice then our differentiation is limited to how we teach and therefore restricted.

Visiting a newly built academy I was impressed by the facilities but concerned that every classroom was set out in exactly the same way: teachers' desks opposite the door, students' desks in rows facing the board. Expecting to meet a dictatorial head who had made a pronouncement on the way in which classes 'should' be laid out I prepared myself for a difficult conversation. It transpired, however, that it was not through a philosophy of teaching that the environment had become so restricted, but because the architects had been allocated 1.5 square metres per child and this was the only way that the desks would fit into the classrooms.

In state education economy is always prioritised over learning, resulting in ICT suites in secondary schools where students are squeezed together and larger students struggle to fit their legs under the bench, automatic temperature controls so that teachers can not open their own windows and classrooms designed with no room for students to put bags so that they either leave them at home or put much less inside.

What we can learn from Victorian schools

Victorian classrooms were not as teacher-led as some would have us believe. The common vision is of one teacher leading from the front and delivering to 40 or more 'empty vessels' eager to be filled with the teacher's knowledge. In truth the organisation of teaching and learning was more personalised and echoes the push for mixed-age teaching and tutor groups we are now experiencing.

The teacher would often instruct the older students on the lesson. He would give them the key learning points, emphasise the key vocabulary and send them off with a small blackboard of ideas to teach small groups of younger students. This might all be done in a large hall with semicircles of students around the 'student teacher'. The older students taught and the teacher toured the groups monitoring the teaching and assessing the learning. Older students took on responsibility for the teaching, as it was unrealistic to expect the large class sizes to receive enough individual attention from one teacher.

Things are not so different today. Class sizes are still inflated and teachers still struggle to give individual students enough attention. Yet asking students to lead teaching and giving responsibility to students for assessing others has been spun as pedagogy that was born in the 1960s by drug-addled liberal teachers who were 'dangerously child centred'. In fact teaching through students is pragmatic rather than political. It is an efficient and sensible use of resources, allows more individual attention, and dispels the myth of the teacher as the only one who is able to teach.

Practical strategies for positive differentiation

- Talk less, give less advice, allow students to do more.
- Use teacher-centred activity for specific tasks such as introducing key concepts, key terminology and phrases and setting learning tasks.

- Aim to absorb students in activities by recognising what they enjoy and respond to best.

- Agree clear simple descriptions of requirement, check understanding and set/ agree clear time periods for each stage of the activity.

- Ensure required targets and outcomes are owned, achievable and capable of stretching the student.

- Mark stage achievement, completion achievement, effort and behaviour.

- Have a source of developmental material available for early completers.

- Ask for student feedback on your teaching. Which questions would you be interested to hear the responses to?

- Rather than being the ringmaster 'controlling' the class be the conductor who connects learning together.

- Look for opportunities for students to take control over the tasks, target, criteria, environment, deadlines and organisation.

Reflecting on practice

Rote learning in Pakistan

I had agreed to go to Peshawar in North West Pakistan before looking at the map. I had agreed to go before I knew that all of the British education consultants had been pulled out some years before. I had agreed to go before knowing that the hotel I was staying in had been bombed the year before and was now inhabited by the CIA and all manner of dubious 'businessmen'. Feeling flattered, foolish and excited I arrived in Pakistan to visit schools, meet headteachers and offer help and guidance where I could.

I had heard that teaching was rooted in rote learning and expected to see lessons with lots of chanting, repetition and memory games. What I found was not what we would understand to be rote learning but a far more basic style. The teacher would stand at the front of the class with a lectern, open a textbook and begin teaching: 'Paris is the capital city of France, the largest country of Western Europe', and the children would repeat 'Paris is the capital city of France, the largest country of Western Europe': 'Paris counts over 2 million inhabitants and is the centre of the 11 million people Paris region', 'Paris counts … '; and so it would continue for 40 minutes until the bell rang and the science teacher came in, put a textbook on the lectern and began the same repetitive ritual of reading out each line with the students repeating them in turn.

Now you might expect that this style of teaching produced poor results. Yet the students were so conditioned, so practised at auditory rote learning (through school as well as through learning Qur'ān at the Mosque) that they were able to process and memorise extremely well. They might not have learned all of the social and study skills that employers would want, but in terms of examination achievement this school had the highest A level pass rate for international A levels in the world. Of course this is selective education. More by money than by ability but selective none the less and there are millions of children in Pakistan who still have no access to free schooling. Yet the achievement is undeniable and all through a pedagogy that most people have forgotten exists.

The students had highly developed individual learning skills but they had not been taught them. The teacher had no interest in differentiation but learning was clearly taking place. The teaching was mechanical, uninspiring and unskilled yet the students were able to pass examinations with the highest grades. This is not an argument for teaching students to parrot information back to the teacher but an acknowledgement that rote learning still has a place. For some areas of learning the ability to recall without reasoning is extremely useful. For some students who are practised in learning by rote outside school we do them a disservice by pretending that their skills are not valuable inside the classroom.

Practical strategies for primary, secondary and further education

Primary

Mind mapping

Teach students mind mapping skills – question maps, maps to tackle specific problems, mapping key points, huge maps on large sheets that everyone contributes to, guides for other students, symbol and image maps, mini maps for thinking in response to a teacher's question.

CVs

Ask students starting your class, tutor group or subject to prepare a personal CV that catalogues their achievements to date. Encourage them to use photographs, examples of work, lists of successes, certificates, etc. As part of termly or annual reviews of work use them as a scrapbook to file ideas, targets, thoughts and memories. Students enjoy designing them and reflecting with them. It also provides an excellent opportunity to embarrass them at leaving dos with photographs of them at a much younger age. Passing on the CVs when they transfer to secondary school also gives the new form tutor a good sense of the personal and academic interests and achievements of the individual.

Secondary

Differentiation

Including differentiation in schemes of work and lesson plans is a thankless task that takes a great deal of time. Use this quick coding to save time, impress the inspectorate and remind yourself of just how many opportunities to differentiate you already have.

The following key can be used in the overview of lessons to signal possible differentiation:

DBG	Differentiation by group (e.g. splitting the class up into groups of similar ability).
DBR	Differentiation by **role** (e.g. students are given a role/responsibility within a group that reflects their ability).
DBT	Differentiation by **task** (e.g. students are given a task that reflects their ability).
DBO	Differentiation by **outcome** (e.g. students are given a target for the task that reflects their ability, i.e. all pupils will have … most pupils will have … and some pupils will have …).
DBTI	Differentiation by **teacher intervention** (e.g. the teacher/LSA gives guidance to students requiring more assistance). This is not mentioned every time it could be used.
DBQ	Differentiation by **questionning** (e.g. the teacher asks more leading, complex questions of the more able).
DBRe	Differentiation by **resource** (e.g. the teacher prepares additional resources to stretch the most able and support the least).
DBF	Differentiation by **follow up** (e.g. students are directed towards appropriate extension materials and media, marking includes target to reach the next level).
DBM	Differentiation by **media** (e.g the teacher uses or guides students to use a range of different media to engage in the activity.

Further education/post-16

Icons

Use icons to code your lesson plans to identify the teaching strategies that you are using to try and embed learning:

Connecting learning

Activating learning

Demonstrating learning

Consolidating learning

Use this four-part cycle from accelerated learning for planning a lesson with opportunities for classroom assessment. You might connect learning to the student's own knowledge and experiences, activate learning through self- and peer assessment, demonstrate by providing a clear model for deconstruction and consolidate through student-led teaching. Use the icons as part of the classroom display to redirect students towards the part of the cycle that they should be working on.

Try icons for other components, such as:

Key skills/vocabulary

Learning competences

Refer to learning competences that you are looking to observe demonstrated, e.g. 'Students would understand how to operate in teams, and their own capacities for filling different team roles' would be an observable and assessable competence.

TOP TIP!

Testing, testing, testing! As each individual processes information and learns differently so each group operates and learns in a unique way. You could spend a great deal of time and energy studying new approaches to learning, trying to calculate which methodology will produce the desired results or you could simply start testing – testing your strategies, trying new ideas, measuring the response, engagement and achievement. Ask students which they prefer and give them the opportunity to provide feedback without fear of offence.

Learning styles, myths and 'myth interpretation'

'I am a kinaesthetic learner, put the pen and paper down and back off!'

The trouble with learning style theory is that by the time it is reinterpreted by busy teachers and reworked by well-meaning consultants the theory is converted into absolutes: 'I am a visual learner and I can not move when I learn'. The truth is that we all have our own preferences for how we learn but they are not constant. They change according to a huge number of variables: content, emotions, relationships, the weather, self-esteem, age.

Many students (and adults) will tell you that they 'have been tested' and are 'visual'. Students are encouraged to use this information to guide you in how to teach them. They rarely use it to reflect on how to improve other areas of learning.

I know that we are trying to move 'traditional teachers' away from didactic teaching and lecturing students but a rounded education could never be achieved by appealing to just one style of learning or one set of preferences. We need to encourage students to examine the ways in which they retain information without pretending that learning preferences are fixed. A more honest approach would be to present learning styles as useful frameworks to test and research but not as scientific or proven.

Exercise

Developing learning conversations

Put the following in order of importance. At the top of your list will be the strategy that promotes most engagement from the student and at the bottom that which promotes the least engagement.

- Giving advice
- Listening
- Explaining
- Training
- Managing
- Feedback
- Appraising

- Directing
- Instruction
- Summarising and reflecting back
- Asking questions
- Analysing
- Evaluating

Giving advice	Coaching
'Tell me exactly what you did'	'It might help if you speak a little more about that?'
'No, the answer you're looking for is six'	'Perhaps tell me how you worked your answer out?'
'You need to open up to me more'	'I notice that you don't always seem to feel comfortable discussing some things with me and I was wondering what caused that?'
'If you want to improve your grades you should work more'	'What is it about your work that you want to improve?'
'Go and join one of those student forums on the internet – they're really helpful'	'What could you do to improve your grades?'
'You're still procrastinating, you simply need to get going'	'What's stopping you from getting into action here?'

Advantages of using non-directive language

- The student is truly listened to and appreciates the effort that is made to understand them.

- The relationship is based on equality, encouraging openness and trust. The teacher is not claiming to have all of the answers and the student feels that their contribution is worthwhile.

- Insights, perspectives and actions come from the student, so does the responsibility for their action and results.

→

- Solutions are developed for the needs of the individual.
- If an idea doesn't get the result that the student wanted the student still has ownership of the idea and so will be more willing to work to get a better result.

Critical questions

- How can you refine your negotiated assessment processes so that they are fully differentiated?
- When can you find time to invest in setting up processes for personal profiling and self-reporting that will, in the medium term, save you time and effort?
- How can you design a reporting system that makes absolute sense to parents and students alike?

Conclusion

Personalising and differentiating assessment to meet the needs of your students does not mean that you have to reinvent your modules of work. Giving students a role in summative recording and reporting further cements their control over their own assessment. Differentiation is not about dumbing down your curriculum but sustaining high expectations while sharpening the emphasis on next step learning for the individual.

Key ideas summary

- Truly personalised learning can not be the sole responsibility of the adults.
- The use of 'statement banks' to create summative reports flies in the face of efforts to personalise and individualise the assessment process.
- Personal profiles are an important part of the assessment process, giving students an opportunity to reflect back on what they have experienced and achieved over the term.
- We spend a great deal of time differentiating our content and significantly less in adjusting the environment so that it is more suited to the needs of the individual.
- Teaching through students is pragmatic rather than political. It is an efficient and sensible use of resources, allows more individual attention and dispels the myth of the teacher as the only one who is able to teach.
- Students who have highly developed skills in learning by rote can be encouraged to utilise these skills in class.

Going further

Mind-mapping: www.mind-mapping.co.uk

How far have we come?

The assessment tree

The fruit on the tree represents the students' autonomous growth. The role of education is to lead students to enter the working world. As we help students to be able to learn independently they can make the transfer with confidence to continue learning for themselves. Empowered with processes that they own and that they use to reflect and improve students can leave education ready to face challenge, failure and success with confidence.

Conclusion

Schools and colleges are not perfect models of education. Students tasked with learning a set curriculum within an institution that inevitably requires conformity and some uniformity doesn't appear to leave room for learning that is owned, personalised and autonomous. But at the classroom level the need to meet the demands of those who persistently fiddle with the curriculum can be balanced with what we know to be best practice.

It is not a revolution that is needed to make education what we want it to be but refinement of what we already do, a sharpening of good practice and a creativity to meet the demands of those who you are accountable to while engaging students to take responsibility for their own learning.

References and additional reading

Bandura, A. (1994) Self-efficacy, in: *Encyclopedia of Human Behavior*, vol. 4, Ramachaudran, V. S. (ed.), Academic Press, pp. 71–81.

Black, P. and Wiliam, D. (1998) *Inside the Black Box*, GL Assessment.

Bloom, B. S. (ed.) (1969) *Taxonomy of Educational Objectives: The Classification of Educational Goals – Handbook 1: Cognitive Domain*, McKay.

Britton, J. (1970) *Language and Learning*, Allen Lane.

Covey, S. R. (1989) *The 7 Habits of Highly Effective People*, Simon and Schuster.

de Bono, E. (1985) *Six Thinking Hats*, available at www.standard.dfes.gov.uk.

Gardner, H. (1993) *Frames of Mind: The Theory of Multiple Intelligences*, 2nd edn, Fontana Press.

Holt, J. (1990) *Why Children Fail*, Penguin.

Jencks, C. (1998) *The Black and White Test Score Gap*, Brookings Institution Press.

Kirkpatrick, D. L. and Kirkpatrick, J. D. (2006) *Evaluating Training Programs*, 3rd edn, Berrett-Koehler.

Krech, G. (2002) *Naikan, Gratitude, Grace and the Japanese Art of Self Reflection*, Stone Bridge Press.

Lewis, C. and Rieman, J. (1994) *Task-Centred User Interface Design: A Practical Introduction*, available at http://hcbib.org/tcuid/tcuid.pdf.

Lutz, A., Brefczynski-Lewis, J., Johnstone, T. and Davidson, R. J. (2008) Regulation of the neural circuitry of emotion by compassion meditation: effects of meditative expertise, *Plos One*, available at www.plosone.org/article/fetchArticle.action?articleURI=info:doi/10.1371/journal.pone.0001897.

Margolis, H. and McCabe, P. (2004) Self-efficacy: a key to improving the motivation of struggling learners, *Clearing House*, vol. 77, no. 6, p. 241.

Medina, J. (2008) *Brain Rules*, Pear Press.

Miller, G. E. (1990) 'The assessment of Clinical Skills Competence/Performance', *Academic Medicine*, 65: 563–7.

Rose, J. (2009) *Independent Review of the Primary Curriculum*, DCSF, available at www.dcsf.gov.uk/primarycurriculumreview.

Rosenthal, R. and Jacobson, L. (1968) *Pygmalion in the Classroom*, Crown House Publishing.

Starr, J. (2003) *The Coaching Manual*, Pearson Education.

Vygotsky, L. S. (1962) *Thought and Language*, MIT Press and John Wiley and Sons.

Index

Page numbers in *italic* denote a diagram/figure

active classroom, managing of 109–19
  exercises 117–18
  and modelling 113
  practical strategies 115–17
  processes 112–13
  and routines 110–12
  and students who are reluctant to peer
    assess 113–14
Assessment for Learning
    QCDA's Ten Principles of 101–3
autonomous learners/learning 17–39, 110
  affording students a voice 23–6
  exercises 35–7
  feedback on teachers 23–5, 38
  giving students responsibility 19–21, 33
  practical strategies 32–4
  and self-reflection 26–8, 32, 38
  and student questioning 29–30
  and teaching formulas 31–2
  and time-management skills 21–3, 33,
    38
  ways to gain student opinion 25–6

backchannelling 68
bad news sandwich 65
Bandura, A. 53, 83
Black, Paul 26
brain 49–52
  changing your 51–2
  creating models of 50
  creatively mapping 50–1
  elasticity of 52
  lobes of *50*
brain hats 56–8
brainstorm 49
Britton, James 42, 97
Brown, Gordon 23
Bush, George W. 80

carousels 75
Challenge Cards *88, 89*
child protection 3
class reports, writing of by students 124
classroom climate 1–15
  and displays 9–11, 14

classroom climate (*continued*)
  emotional 3–7, 14
  exercise 13
  impact of finding fault 6
  physical 9–11
  practical strategies 11–13
  risk-taking by students 7–8, 12, 14
  setting of by teacher 3–4
  and teacher-student relationship 2–3,
      12–13
classrooms
  layout 127–8
  managing active assessment in 109–19
  metacognitive 42
  size of 122, 128
  Victorian 128
coaching 29
coloured thinking hats (de Bono) 27–8,
    35–6, 38
communication
  between student and teacher 11
  encouraging of conservation through
      oracy frames 104–6
  ways to facilitate productive learning
      conversations 103–4, 134–5
competencies 45–7, *46*
computer-generated reports 123–4, 135
conscious competence/incompetence 45
conscious unconscious competence 45
conversations
  extending of through oracy frames
      104–6
  ways to facilitate productive learning
      103–4, 134–5
'Counting to 20' game 12
Covey, Stephen
  time-management quadrants 21, *22*
criteria
  developing student lists of 122–3
  NAGs and defining success 96–7, 106
  understanding examination/level 48–9,
      61
criticism
  impact of on classroom climate 6
CVs 130–1

Davidson, Richard 51
de Bono, E.
  coloured thinking hats 27–8, 35–6, 38
  Thinking Skills 55
deadlines 21, 22
differentiation of assessment *see*
      personalisation/differentiation of
      assessment
digital photo frames 9, 10
displays, classroom 9–11, 14

Elliot, Jane 83
emotional environment (classroom) 3–7,
    14
emotions
  impact of assessment on 6, 14, 102
  learning of positive 51
  and self-efficacy 53
  and targets/target setting 81–2, 93
expectations, student
  and targets 83–8

failure 4, 5
fault finding 6
FE strategies *see* post-16 strategies
feedback 11, 103
  3:1 6, 14, 65, 87
  and the internet 23
  and peer assessment 65, 67–8, 69
  and targets/target setting 87
  on teachers by students 23–5, 38
fortune tellers
  developing and extending peer
      conversations with 72–4
four-line plays 75–6
functional magnetic resonance imaging
    (fMRI) 51

Gardner, Howard
  intrapersonal intelligence 26
  multiple intelligences 55, 59
Glasser, William 7, 60
group work 4
  defining spaces for 115

Hendrix, Jimi 64
Holt, John 18
homework
    and self-study 34
    student feedback on 24

icons
    use of to code lesson plans 131–2
ICT 127
inspectorate 42–3
    and target setting 80
insurance executives (case study) 116–17
intelligence(s)
    intrapersonal 26
    multiple 55, 59
internet 23
intrapersonal intelligence 26
introspection 26

Japanese Art of Self Reflection 27
Japanese Reiki 32
Jencks, C.
    The Black and White Test Score Gap
        83–4
Jordan, Michael 6
Jung, Carl 110

language
    extending conversations through oracy
        frames 104–6
    strategies to facilitate productive learning
        conversations 103–4, 134–5
learning
    as non quantifiable 42–3, 61
learning maps/journeys 5
learning styles 133
    questionnaires 49
lesson bullets 34
lesson plans
    three-part 30–1
    use of icons to code 131–3
Lewis, Clayton 54
listening
    and peer assessment 68–9

mantras, daily 32
Margolis, H. and McCabe, P. 53
marking
    of each other's work by students 66–7
martial arts 45
mastery experiences 53
maths
    extending conversations through oracy
        frames 104–5
memory 43
metacognition/metacognitive skills 29–30,
        41–62
    and competences 45–6, 46
    exercises 60
    gaining self-efficacy by students 53–4
    habits and rituals 43–4
    and learning styles questionnaires 49
    meaning 42
    and mobile phones 47–8
    practical strategies 56–9
    and study skills 52
    Thinkenstein project 54–6
    thinking about the brain 49–52
    understanding examination/level criteria
        48–9
metacognitive spinners 58
mind map/mapping 49, 130
mind shower 49
mobile phones 61
    and metacognition 47–8
modelling 113
multiple intelligences 55, 59
music
    and self-reflection 28
Muslim culture 70–1

NAGs (Negotiated Assessment Grids) 55,
        95–107
    benefits 96
    defining success criteria to assess skills
        96–7, 106
    educational purposes of 101
    and QCDA's Ten Principles of Assessment
        for Learning 101–3
    ways to use 99–100

Naikan Self-reflection 27
Neelands, Jonathan 96
Negotiated Assessment Grids *see* NAGs
NQT 110

oracy frames, extending conversations
          through 104–6
Orwell, George 122

Pakistan
    rote learning in 129–30
paraphrasing 69
'parent on the shoulder' 3
parents
    involving in target setting 91
peer assessment 5, 63–77
    attitude of students 64
    benefits 64
    exercises 75–6
    and feedback 65, 67–8, 69
    and fortune tellers 72–4
    and listening 68–9
    managing students who show reluctance
        in 113–14
    marking each other's work 66–7
    and Muslim culture 70–1
    practical strategies 71–4
    presentations and performances 67–8
    problems associated with 64
    and rituals/routines 65–6
    scoring systems 71
    setting a strong model 65–6, 76
personal assessment profiles 124–6, 135
personalisation/differentiation of
          assessment 122–36
    and classroom layout 127–8
    and computer-generated reports 123–4,
        135
    exercises 134–5
    and personal assessment profiles 124–6,
        135
    practical strategies 128–9, 130–3
    student criteria lists 122–3
    writing of class reports by students 124
personalised learning 18, 38, 122

physical environment (classroom) 9–11
Pivotal's Negotiated Assessment Grids *see*
          NAGs
positive reinforcement 5, 34, 111
post-16 strategies
    autonomous learning 34
    classroom climate 12–13
    managing active classrooms 116
    metacognitive thinking 59
    peer assessment 72
    personalisation and differentiation of
        assessment 131–3
    targets/target setting 91
PowerPoint 8, 127
prayer 26
presentations/performances
    and peer assessment 67–8
primary school strategies
    autonomous learning 32–3
    classroom climate 11
    managing active classrooms 115
    metacognitive thinking 56–8
    peer assessment 72
    personalisation and differentiation of
        assessment 130–1
    targets/target setting 88–9

QCDA
    Ten Principles of Assessment for Learning
        101–3
questioning, metacognitive 42
questionnaires, learning styles 49
questions
    encouraging children to take a risk when
        answering 7–8
    for younger students to use for self-
        reflection 32
    promotion of autonomous learning
        through dealing with student 29–30

racism study (Elliot) 83
rapport 3
refining work 33
relationships
    between teacher and student 2–3,
        12–13, 112

reports
  computer-generated summative 123–4, 135
  writing of class reports by students 124
respect 3
responsibility, giving of to students 19–21, 33
rewards 8
risk-taking, by students in the classroom 7–8, 13, 14
rituals
  and peer assessment 65–6
road maps 5
Rose, J. 43
Rosenthal, R. and Jacobsen, L.
  Pygmalion in the Classroom 83
rote learning (Pakistan) 129–30
routines
  and managing active classrooms 110–12
  and peer assessment 65–6
rules 112

scorecards
  and peer assessment 72
seating plans 12, 64
secondary school strategies
  autonomous learning 33
  classroom climate 11–12
  managing active classrooms 116
  metacognitive thinking 58–9
  peer assessment 72–4
  personalisation and differentiation of assessment 131
  targets/target setting 89–91
self-efficacy
  ways for students to gain 53–4
self-esteem 7
self-fulfilling prophecy 84, *84*
self-reflection 26–8, 38
  balanced 27, 38
  and de Bono's coloured thinking hats 27–8
  and intrapersonal intelligence 26
  Japanese Art of 27
  questions for younger students to use for 32

self-study
  helping students to plan 22
  and homework 34
SMART targets 82, 93
speaking and listening work 103–5
  and maths 104–5
special mission cards *88, 89*
spinners, metacognitive 58
statement banks 123, 135
string, use of to define spaces for group work 115
student observation sheet 24–5
students
  answering questions from 29–30
  as autonomous learners *see* autonomous learners/learning
  encouraging of to gauge own abilities 45–6
  gaining self-efficacy 53–4
  marking each other's work 66–7
  negotiating with 112
  and peer assessment *see* peer assessment
  relationship with teachers 2–3, 12–13, 112
  risk-taking in the classroom 7–8, 13, 14
  teaching through 12, 128, 135
  treating of as adults 12
  ways to gain opinion from 25–6
  writing of own class reports 124
study skills 52
summative reports, computer-generated 123–4, 135

target maps *90*
target setting days 85
targets/target setting 32, 79–94
  drawing of 87–8
  and emotions 81–2, 93
  exercises 91–2
  features of that impact on achievement 81
  and feedback 87
  ideas for improving discussions on 85–6
  and inspectorate 80
  involving parents in 91
  as meaningful to students 82–3

targets/target setting (*continued*)
 and NAGs 98
 overload and prioritising of 86
 practical strategies 88–91
 and self-fulfilling prophecy 84, *84*
 SMART 82, 93
 and student expectations 83–8, 93
TASC model 55, *55*
teachers
 changing habits 111–12
 as learner model 4–5, 11, 14
 managing active classrooms *see* active
  classrooms, managing of
 negotiating with students 112
 relationship with students 2–3,
  12–13, 112
 setting of classroom climate 3–4
 student feedback on 23–5, 38
 and target setting 80
teaching formulas 31–2
testing 18
think aloud protocol 54

think, pair, share 71
Thinkenstein project 54–6
thinking hats (de Bono) 27–8, 35–6, 38
thinking posts 59
3:1 feedback 6, 14, 65, 87
time-management skills 21–3, 33, 38
traffic light symbols 8, 11
tree analogy, and assessment 2
trust, building mutual 3, 12–13

unconscious competence/incompetence 45

verbal persuasion 53
vicarious experience 53
Victorian classrooms 128
Vygotsky, L.S. 104

Wallace, Belle
 TASC model 55, 55
William, Dylan 26
Wragg, Ted 96

Classroom Gems

Innovative resources, inspiring creativity across the school curriculum

Designed with busy teachers in mind, the Classroom Gems series draws together an extensive selection of practical, tried-and-tested, off-the-shelf ideas, games and activities, guaranteed to transform any lesson or classroom in an instant.

Primary Modern Foreign Languages

© 2008 Paperback 336pp
ISBN: 9781405873925

Primary Classroom

© 2008 Paperback 312pp
ISBN: 9781405859455

Primary PE
Will Allen

© 2009 Paperback 224pp
ISBN: 9781408220382

Learning Outside the Primary Classroom
Paul Barron

© 2009 Paperback 256pp
ISBN: 9781408225608

Primary Mathematics
John Dabell

© 2009 Paperback 304pp
ISBN: 9781408223208

Primary Humanities
Richard Green

© 2009 Paperback 304pp
ISBN: 9781408228098

Primary Music
Donna Minto

© 2009 Paperback 304pp
ISBN: 9781408223260

Primary Drama
Michael Theodorou

© 2009 Paperback 304pp
ISBN: 9781408223291

Early Years Phonics
Lynn Cousins and Gill Coulson

© 2009 Paperback 304pp
ISBN: 9781408224359

Secondary Classroom
Mark Lebrow

© 2009 Paperback 256pp
ISBN: 9781408225578

Primary Science
John Dabell

© 2010 Paperback 304pp
ISBN: 9781408223239

Primary Literacy
Hazel Glynne and Amanda Snowden

© 2010 Paperback 336pp
ISBN: 9781408225516

'Easily navigable, allowing teachers to choose the right activity quickly and easily, these invaluable resources are guaranteed to save time and are a must-have tool to plan, prepare and deliver first-rate lessons'

Longman
is an imprint of

PEARSON

The Essential Guides Series

Practical skills for teachers

The Essential Guides series offers a wealth of practical support, inspiration and guidance for NQTs and more experienced teachers ready to implement into their classroom. The books provide practical advice and tips on the core aspects of teaching and everyday classroom issues, such as planning, assessment, behaviour and ICT. The Essential Guides are invaluable resources that will help teachers to successfully navigate the challenges of the profession.

The Essential Guide to
Secondary Teaching
Susan Davies

© 2010 paperback
ISBN 978-1-4082-2452-6

The Essential Guide to
Using ICT Creatively in the Primary Classroom
Steve Woods

© 2010 paperback
ISBN 978-1-4082-2497-7

The Essential Guide to
Taking Care of Behaviour
(second edition)
Paul Dix

© 2010 paperback
ISBN 978-1-4082-2554-7

The Essential Guide to
Successful School Trips
John Trant

© 2010 paperback
ISBN 978-1-4082-0447-4

The Essential Guide to
Understanding Special Educational Needs
Jenny Thompson

© 2010 paperback
ISBN 978-1-4082-2500-4

The Essential Guide to
Shaping Children's Behaviour in the Early Years
Lynn Cousins

© 2010 paperback
ISBN 978-1-4082-2502-8

The Essential Guide to
Teaching 14-19 Diplomas
Lynn Senior

© 2010 paperback
ISBN 978-1-4082-2549-3

Longman is an imprint of

PEARSON

Practical skills for teachers